From G
to Gratitude

Catriona Whyte

SPERO HOUSE

Published in 2024 by Spero House

Copyright © Catriona Whyte 2024

Catriona Whyte has asserted her right to be identified as the author of this Work in accordance with the Copyright, Designs and Patents Act 1988

ISBN Paperback: 978-1-0687134-0-8
Ebook: 978-1-0687134-1-5

All rights reserved. No part of this publication may be reproduced, stored in a retrieval system, or transmitted in any form or by any means, electronic, mechanical, photocopying, recording or otherwise, without the prior permission of the copyright owner.

A CIP catalogue copy of this book can be found in the British Library.

Published with the help of Indie Authors World
www.indieauthorsworld.com

This book is dedicated to my mum and dad. They never had the chance to be a part of my journey through adulthood, but their unconditional love remains etched in my heart forever.

With special thanks to Graham, for always being there, for your continuous support and love. And to our beautiful daughter Katie, the greatest gift we've ever been given. She teaches and inspires us every day.

Author's Note

While this book recounts real-life events. I have altered the names of the patients I cared for to protect their identity and privacy within the narrative.

Introduction

The year 1990 heralded a new decade and era. That summer, as I turned eighteen, I gained the legal privileges of drinking alcohol and going to nightclubs. However, I had already been indulging in both activities, thanks to a fake ID I obtained from a friend's dad. Every weekend, amid my school exam preparations, you could find me at the Cue Ball nightclub, within staggering distance of my home in Victoria Road, on the southside of Glasgow. The anticipation and excitement of getting ready were integral to the nights experience. With my hair backcombed and excessively sprayed, it added a few inches to my petite frame. I adored the euphoric sensation of entering amidst booming music, vibrating through my core, eagerly anticipating the chance to strut my stuff on the dancefloor.

The Happy Mondays, Black box, The B-52's and many other bands and songs evoke memories of those carefree and joyful times. I used to party there with Colette, my closest friend from school. We regularly encountered familiar faces and crushes. It was during those weekends that I formed lifelong unwavering and supportive friendships with Susan and Tracy. I loved many different genres of music, pop music, country & western and power ballads. I was a superfan of Madonna, Whitney, Cher and Dolly, legends that didn't even require a surname.

Glasgow was an up-and-coming city, and it became the European City of Culture in 1990. This was a proud achievement, for a place which is known both for its friendliness and its violence. It catapulted the city into a place where the arts and culture were really celebrated and embraced, rather than just being known for its tough streets and poverty. Scotland's football team had also made it to Italia 1990, the World Cup, a glorious achievement. Qualifying for major championships is something we Scots don't get the opportunity to experience often, despite our passionate support for the magical game.

A whole new world awaited me. I finished school that summer at Holyrood, the largest Secondary school in Scotland. I began my student nurse training on August 6th, 1990, only 4 weeks before the early morning call that changed everything….

CHAPTER 1

One Moment in Time

6th September 1990. 06.00 am.
The piercing rings of the telephone shattered the morning silence. My Mum answered.

> *"Hello, is that Mrs McLennan? It's the staff nurse from Ward 17. I'm calling to tell you Albert's condition has deteriorated. Can you make your way to the hospital right away?"*

A single call, a solitary moment that forever altered the trajectory of my family's life.

While my mum and my eldest sister Christine headed to the hospital, my other, older sister Yvonne, her two-year-old daughter Laura and I stayed at home. I got dressed and ready for nursing college, on autopilot with the song "Don't give up" by Peter Gabriel and Kate Bush playing on the radio. We waited, anxious for news, for what seemed like an eternity. Hearing the key turn in the door, we congregated by the piano in the hallway, a place where we had spent our childhood learning to play. "*He's gone.*" The weight of those words lingered heavily in the air.

My Dad had died before they reached the hospital ward. He was only 60 years old. *"Don't leave us Mum"* I sobbed, as I fell into her arms. I knew I was losing her too. She had been diagnosed four months previously with cancer in both of her lungs. Only seven months later she died, on the 17th of April 1991.

*

Losing my parents in such close proximity to each other at a young age, and particularly the death of my mum has had a profound impact throughout my life. Even in those early days of coping with my grief and despite my losses, I had a deep sense of gratitude for being brought up in a happy and loving environment. I knew how different my life could have been as I had been adopted.

The weight of those two significant losses inflicted both physical and emotional anguish upon me, making me intimately familiar with the sensation of a broken heart. Despite those months and years of grief and sadness, I have so many happy memories too. I had fun and freedom, and I was in a job that I loved. I can honestly say that Nursing saved me. It gave me an additional new family of close friends who loved and supported me, and I am grateful for the lasting friendships and vibrant social life that my career provided me. Providing care to others and truly impacting the lives of sick patients and their families brought immense fulfilment.

Throughout my early adult life, I was exposed to many challenges personally and professionally. I began to experience physical and mental health issues, none of which I particularly understood at the time. A breakdown in my thirties prompted action. I needed help and a change in lifestyle. I had never properly acknowledged my grief and, as the years rolled by, I began to experience burnout. I didn't realise that by not looking after myself and burying my sadness and guilt, I was becoming sick, physically, emotionally and spiritually. Slowly, I started to understand the significance of the body and mind connection.

I experienced loss, grief, joy and happiness, seemingly opposite things, all at the same time and for an extended period I slowly began to navigate my way through the fog. Finding tools along the way to help me onto a journey of self-discovery. The transformations took place over a long period and during that time I began to realise that the most vital connection I would ever make, didn't lie in others but with myself.

Most particularly, I learnt the utmost importance of self-care, of self-love, of having gratitude for all that I had, rather than concentrating on all that was lost. This awakening came to me when I discovered the transformative healing powers of Reiki. As I progress through my journey, I continuously uncover that I am evolving and growing. I'm a work in progress. I've also come to understand that, regardless of our backgrounds, environment, and life experiences, we all require tools to navigate this life. Through love, hope and gratitude, I've discovered that anything is possible.

CHAPTER 2

The Early Years

It was never a secret from my mum and dad, that my sisters Christine and Yvonne and I were adopted from different families. Like all siblings, we argued and disagreed, but I wouldn't have changed them or my childhood for the world. I don't recall any feelings of anger or resentment towards my birth mum, just a deep sense of gratitude of being part of the family unit that I was in.

The three of us were all told from a young age that we were special and chosen. It was spoken about openly and because I was given so much love from our parents, I never had any desire to search for my birth family. I never felt that anything was missing from my life, although I have a vague recollection of being about fifteen and feeling at times that I didn't belong. I think that can be an age for a lot of kids to have feelings like mine though, regardless of their circumstances.

Having said this, I consider myself extremely lucky as I recognise that everyone's experience of adoption will be different and there is no right or wrong way to feel. Some people, regardless of whether they perceive themselves as having a good childhood or not, still have that inherent need to find out more. It doesn't mean if a person wishes to trace their birth family that they are unhappy, we are just all different.

My own personal belief is that as I am adopted and unaware of my roots, I am a blank canvas. I chose to look at that always as a positive. Yes, my biology has genetically determined many things. My sex, my eye colour, skin pigmentation, perhaps my temperament and some other behavioural aspects that I don't know or maybe understand. Just as importantly though is the learning from my upbringing and its core values. My mum and dad taught me me how to love and be loved. Love is the greatest gift of all. Everything I did throughout my life, without me fully realising it at the time was driven from a place of love.

When my husband Graham and I started planning for our own family, I longed for my mum. She would have understood the fertility struggles I faced and the joy when the dream came true. I thought a lot more about my birth mum throughout that time, and how traumatic it must have been for her to give me away.

My mum's depth of gratitude and empathy for our birth-mothers was beautiful and gracious. Every year my mum would light a candle on our birthdays for all of them to thank them for that gift of motherhood for her. I never forgot that, and I have carried on that tradition by lighting a candle for my birth mum on my birthday now. I'm aware that the likelihood is that my birth was a secret that was never shared with others. I was born in the seventies, and at that time and for decades before, there was a terrible stigma associated with babies being born out of wedlock in Ireland and Britain. Babies were some-times taken away cruelly without any emotional support for the young mums, which is incredibly sad and wrong. Some, I am sure were still children or barely adults themselves. Like everything in life, there is at least two sides to a story. The desperation and pain that comes with such a momentous decision, and the joy that is given to those desperate to have children of their own. I am forever grateful to my birth mother for the life I was given and for the life I have lived with my family.

Many people, when I told them I was adopted would ask if I ever had wanted to trace my real parents but, my real mum was Rebecca, not the mum who gave birth to me. She was the one who loved and nurtured me in a home where I felt happy and safe. Albert, who taught me so much, about courage, resilience, social justice, and had a wicked sense of humour, that was my real dad.

I hope my birth mum found peace with her decision, as undoubtedly it stayed with her for the rest of her life. I can only imagine how that painful choice, borne out of love would have impacted her.

*

My family moved to Victoria Road on the Southside of Glasgow with my sisters, before I became part of the family in 1972. They came from a room and kitchen tenement flat in Govanhill. It had been a tight squeeze, with all four of them sharing a small room. There was a communal toilet outside the flat (or as it's referred to in Glasgow, the close) on the landing, so a move to a large three bedroomed tenement flat with an internal bathroom would have been sheer luxury. We had everything quite literally on our doorstep, a newsagent, fish and chip shop, off licence and the famous Queens Café ice cream parlour and the Anarkali Indian restaurant. Both of which have stood the test of time and still remain popular!

I spent many summers in the Queens Park, a hop, skip and a jump away. The park was developed in the late 19th century because of the ever-rising population on the Southside. It provided green spaces for people away from their houses. It was dedicated to the memory of Mary, Queen of Scots and steeped in history. It had several swing parks, a boating pond, tennis courts, and a bandstand to name a few. The views across Glasgow from the flagpole were amazing and you can see Ben Lomond and the Campsie Fells on a clear day. I hung around a lot with Yvonne, my middle sister, as there was an eight-year age gap with me and Christine but only four between Yvonne and me. We had great times growing up together, playing in the park, such fun and carefree times. My favourite memories are the many summer holidays at the organised camps. The games started in the morning and went on throughout the day. We played, competed in obstacle courses and sang a lot of songs. The only song I can remember was "This is the Day" and to this day, whenever I hear it, it makes me smile.

However, as with every family, there were sad memories from my childhood as well. One night my dad's mum called, to tell him that his dad had died. I probably didn't really understand at the time what was happening, I was only four, but I sensed his sadness and pain. It was a dark and frosty night in January; he stood alone at the bus stop, while I watched from the living room window. My granda had died suddenly of a heart attack, my gran, died the following September. Little did I imagine that history would repeat itself, just over a decade later with our own parents. My dad died on the same day as his own mum had, twelve years later. Both with pneumonia along with other health complications.

Throughout my childhood, there was a lot of hospital admissions for both my parents. My mum was first diagnosed with cancer when I was ten years old, she had bowel cancer and spent a while in hospital having surgery to remove the tumour. She then spent a period of time recuperating in Mearnskirk hospital in Newton Mearns on the outskirts of Glasgow. Yvonne was apparently put in charge of doing the washings. Dad wasn't used to doing any household chores, like many a man of his time. However, I think he may have taken umbridge to the fact my Mum didn't trust him to do it. He told Yvonne she could go out with her pals as he was perfectly capable. The result being our school uniforms shrinking in a boil wash! I don't remember being worried or stressed when my mum was in hospital, although no doubt I missed her being at home, but I remember that incident clearly! The question on everybody's lips was *"Who is telling mum?"*

My mum was diagnosed again with cancer around five years later, this time in her bladder, resulting in further hospital stays. Again, she had surgery and made a good recovery, or so we thought…

My sisters and I were shielded, like so many in society at that time, compared to nowadays where kids are exposed to so much, particularly through social media. Although, on the occasion when someone exposed themselves to me and a friend in our tenement close on route to a football match, at Hampden Park nearby, they didn't bargain for my wee mum. She chased him with her slipper! She may have been petite and polite but if you messed with her family, she had the roar of a lion.

Being the youngest, I probably got away with a lot more than my two sisters although it didn't feel like that at the time. My mum was in her late fifties when I became a teenager, so she had learnt a lot by then, especially I think, when it came to choosing her battles and what really mattered.

As with every family there were several incidents growing up with my sisters that caused upset and concern at the time but as adults we now look back on and laugh about, most of which involved items of clothing.

I borrowed, or should I say stole several of Yvonnes clothes on different occasions, but I always managed to get caught out. Wearing her prized blue and white diamond patterned Pringle jumper to school was my first faux pas. During the home economics class, the teacher cried out *"something is burning"* I looked around to see who had burnt their food, only to realise it was indeed the precious Pringle jumper that was on fire. Luckily no injuries were sustained, but all that was really left of the jumper was the back and the sleeves!

The next incident however was slightly more dramatic and life threatening. I was fifteen years old and again borrowed something from Yvonne. This time a mustard-coloured jacket of hers, along with a pair of brand-new navy trousers for me, which had been hidden away in my mum's wardrobe as part of my upcoming Christmas present. As I ran to the bus stop bus outside my friend's house on a busy main road in the bucketing rain…BANG!

I still remember that noise and the impact. I was catapulted into the air by a car and onto the bonnet of another, then onto the ground. I lay there stunned. The paramedics and police arrived quickly. It had been totally my fault; I wasn't looking where I was going. The paramedic shouted above the noise of the traffic. *"Does anyone know her name"*. I think they were surprised that I could respond. Despite the knock to my head, I hadn't lost consciousness, and I was completely aware of what was going on and able to give my details. *"Where does it hurt?" "My head and right leg."*

The next noise was the unmistakable ripping of the trousers to check for injuries. I burst into floods of tears. The paramedics kindly reassured and comforted me, assuming I was distressed by the incident. I don't think they expected me to say: *"My sister is going to kill me, I have her jacket on, and these are my Christmas trousers"*.

Thankfully an x ray and scan at the hospital confirmed no damage, no broken bones, how lucky was I not to have sustained any serious damage. The police went to my house to inform my parents, and the nurse in Accident and Emergency told me my sister was coming for me, I cried out *"Which one?"* Luckily it was Christine, and due to the sheer relief on everyone's part that I was not seriously injured was the only reason I got away with that one.

CHAPTER 3

A Father's Love

My dad had COPD, (Chronic Obstructive Pulmonary Disease), which is the name for a group of lung conditions that cause difficulties with breathing. It includes emphysema (damage to the air sacs in the lungs) and chronic bronchitis (long term inflammation of the airways) He was also a Type 1 diabetic which meant he required insulin twice daily.

He left school at fourteen and became a lift engineer and electrician, but unfortunately had to retire early due to ill health. His main trips laterally consisted of being escorted to hospital in the back of an ambulance. He was well known amongst the paramedics and their kindness and professionalism were always much appreciated as his fragile health meant he would often deteriorate rapidly. Their impact was so great that I seriously considered a job in the ambulance service.

When my dad and I talked through possible career options, he suggested I would make a great nurse. He was so proud of me when I was accepted into nursing the year before he died. I am grateful, not only that he encouraged me to consider it as an option, but that he got to see me start my nursing, albeit briefly. It played a significant part in my life for so long.

Despite suffering poor health with his chronic medical conditions, I remember fondly the days of doing spelling battles with him and naming the capitals of countries. He was a whizz at general knowledge and would often help with homework. He took a great interest in me and in what we all did, he was very encouraging, and he just wanted us to try our best.

How hard that must have been for my dad to be virtually housebound in his fifties due to the progression of his illness and to lose that sense of contact with the outside world. I reflected on this a lot through the pandemic when we were all in lockdown. His only real visitor apart from family was Ritchie, a young apprentice who he had worked with and took under his wing. I don't ever know what happened to Ritchie, but I appreciate just how important those visits were now I am older. I have a much greater understanding of the loneliness and isolation he must have felt.

From an early age I knew how to take my dad's blood sugars to monitor his diabetes. It was sometimes quite frightening, as he would turn verbally aggressive if his blood sugars were too low, a symptom known as hypoglycaemia. He would sometimes be aware himself that he was becoming hypoglycaemic, but more often than not it was discovered when we noticed a change in his behaviour or when his blood sugars were being checked routinely before mealtimes.

When he was still working, he enjoyed his times at the pub, as did we, as he would come home merry on pay day with treats. This was usually fish and chips, a bottle of fizzy juice and a chocolate bar each. When he developed his diabetes and he could no longer go to the pub, he then lost that hugely important social connection which he loved and that must have been very hard for him.

Sadly, his health started to deteriorate six or or seven years before he died, and he was unable to work at all, although I genuinely can't remember him ever complaining. He eventually become a shadow of his former self. I found that very difficult, watching my strong, hardworking dad who had served in the army, losing weight and muscle mass. When my mum worked on a Saturday, I was on dad duty. I have such fond memories of watching Match of the Day with him and going out for the shopping. This involved going to lots of different shops to get the cheapest deals, and I always managed a wee trip to RS McColl's newsagents for Callard and Bowsers, delicious toffees which I can still taste and smell when I think of them, and American Cream Soda. This of course was not part of a diabetic diet, but it was my dad's and my treat (and secret!)

*

My dad was admitted to Ward 17 of the Victoria Infirmary, a teaching hospital in the Battlefield/Langside area of Glasgow, in August 1990, shortly after I began my student nurse training. I was used to him being an inpatient, so, I didn't see this as different to any other admission. I never imagined it would be his last. When I look back over the years, as you inevitably do, I wondered did my dad realise how unwell he was? Could we have done more? My last treasured time I spent with him was on my own at the evening visit two nights before he died. He was perhaps quieter than usual, and did I imagine it, or did we hold each other that wee bit tighter for what was to be the last time?

I realise now that my dad had finally given up, all the years of poor health, struggling for breath, losing his independence and the final straw of my mum's terminal illness. As hard as it was to lose both my parents, only seven months apart, I know my dad couldn't have lived without my mum. I fully believe that it was meant to be that he died first.

I never got to properly grieve for my dad at the time of his death because my mum then immediately started to decline. Years later, and with all the experiences of nursing patients with similar conditions to my dad's, I started to recognise the effect that the lung disease had on his quality of life. He was so brave. I felt guilty that I didn't get to know more about him. It's only when you get older, you realise that your parents are not just your mum or dad, but individuals with their own histories and experiences. Like all of us as human beings, they weren't perfect, they sometimes got it wrong but in the main, they did things with the best intentions. My dad absolutely loved politics and he had a strong sense of justice. He was involved with strike action in the late seventies, standing alongside other workers, protesting about poor pay and conditions. This was known as the winter of discontent throughout the UK in 1978/79. Unfortunately, there are parallels that can be drawn with what happened then with what is happening now in the UK.

I know some of the traits I have taken from my dad are to stand up for what I believe in and the utmost importance of fairness in society. He never lost his sense of identity, and he was very proud of his northern Scottish Aberdeen working class roots. For many years after his death, I felt I had let him down. If I had a bad experience with a relative or patient, these guilty feelings would emerge, and I would take negative issues very personally. I would think if I had failed a relative or patient, then I had failed him also. Counselling showed me later in life that I put absolutely everything physically and psychologically into my job, partly because I was trying to make up for the guilt of not looking after my dad and mum at home.

CHAPTER 4

A Mother's Love

My mum was diagnosed in April 1990 with lung cancer, secondaries from her previous bladder and bowel cancers just as I was finishing my sixth-year exams. I remember the day she told me and my dad as if it were yesterday. She broke the news on a Friday afternoon after seeing the GP. She had been troubled with a continuous cough for several months. Only later, looking back on photographs could I see how thin she had become. Christine had just got married and was away on honeymoon.

My mum came home from the Doctors practice and asked my dad and I to sit down at the kitchen table. I will never forget the utter devastation on my dad's face, he just put his head in his hands. I know a part of him died that day too. My mum's GP was unfortunately quite cruel in the way he conveyed the diagnosis to her, which stayed with me for a long time. She sat in the surgery alone receiving the news and then walked home in a daze. His way of telling her was to say. *"Sorry to spoil your weekend, but you have cancer in both lungs."*

I don't remember the next few months in any great detail; I turned eighteen in the July and then I started my student nursing in the August. The next few months I carried on with my training, watching my beloved mum becoming increasingly weaker, thinner and breathless. She missed my dad so much and I struggled with her grief as well as my own. I found myself going to the pub a lot after work, a normal thing for a student to do but something that later left me with a tremendous sense of guilt for leaving her and enjoying myself. I remember regularly going into my mum's bed, listening to the rasping of her breath, gently feeling her pulse, terrified she would die. She slept for the most part of her remaining months, in the living room, as it was easier for her breathing to lie in a more upright position.

She received palliative radiotherapy to help manage her symptoms of breathlessness, but she only tolerated a few sessions, she was simply too weak to continue, and she was experiencing intense nausea and sickness. In her final weeks and days, she was seen by the Macmillan Team and the same GP that had given her her terminal diagnosis. My brave wee mum did in fact tell him she had been devastated, not only with her prognosis the previous year, but by the words he had used and being alone to face this news. He did apologise, which gave some comfort, but it made me realise at this early stage in my career as a nurse, that our words and the way we are with people, particularly when they are receiving bad news, has a significant impact on their grief.

It took a long time for me to forgive that Doctor and I chose not to see him personally after that as a patient. However, I am also aware of positive experiences that other individuals had with him and at the end of the day he was human. Maybe he just didn't know how to convey that diagnosis, as looking back he was probably a relatively young GP at the time. Perhaps my mum's words hopefully helped him to be more compassionate in his own words and way of being with others.

I don't remember having any conversations with my mum about her dying and even though deep down I knew she would, there was that hope, maybe a miracle that she would survive. However, on Thursday 10th April 1991, my mum was admitted to the Prince and Princess of Wales Hospice in the city centre of Glasgow as she had reached the stage where she required oxygen and specialist care. I was left in the house on my own after the ambulance crew took her away. Yvonne was working, Laura, her daughter was at nursery school and it just hit me, an overwhelming sadness and quietness. My Mum said as she was leaving. *"I will only be in there a week."* I don't know if she knew she was dying or whether she thought she would return home, but she was indeed only there a week, dying peacefully the following Thursday on the 17th of April. She was 62 years old.

The Hospice staff were wonderful, and this had a profound impact on me. I saw how the doctors and nurses cared for her and I realised then that communication, empathy and honesty is so important. On the morning that she died, we were called in, early in the morning. The ward sister Ruby had taken me aside and explained in a gentle way that my mum didn't have long and encouraged us to say anything we wanted to say to her, which we did individually. I thanked my Mum for adopting me and for her love, before she slipped into unconsciousness. We sat with her for many hours. She slipped away with Yvonne at her bedside. Christine and I had popped out for some fresh air, something again which I felt guilty about and desperately wish I could have changed.

I think my mum wasn't so much frightened of dying but of leaving us so soon after dad. She had a strong faith and believed in God's love, taking great comfort from her final visit from the priest when she was given the sacraments of the sick. This is the final sacrament given in the Catholic Church at the time of great illness or when death is near.

The compassion and dignity that my mum and we, as a family experienced from the hospice staff was comforting and touched us all. I am to this day extremely grateful for the care she received. I believe these events, although traumatic and at times unbearable helped shape me as a nurse and as an individual. Maybe it was always meant to be, that for most of my nursing career, I would end up caring for people at the end of their lives with lung disease. I didn't nurse my own mum and dad, but I tried my utmost every day to care and provide comfort to other peoples' parents and families. I felt so much for people during this pandemic who were not given the opportunity to be with their loved ones. This must have been unbearable.

*

I had a special relationship with my mum which I have always cherished. We were very affectionate with each other, and I really struggled for a long time without her. She was always there, going home for lunch every day in both primary and secondary school. She made great Halloween costumes, my favourite of which won the prize at the brownies. I was Maid Marion, the heroine of the Robin Hood legend in English folklore. Creating imaginative costumes is certainly not a skill that I have inherited from her with my own daughter unfortunately. Despite the frequent hospital admissions and ill health for both my parents, the fondest memories of my childhood are being at the Brownies, Guides and in the Church choir. I can remember many happy times at the Brownies in particular, the shows and the sense of fun in working towards a new badge. I have a particularly strong memory of trudging up to the Battlefield monument at Langside in the bucketing rain, to copy down the words from the inscription on the memorial there. This commemorates the Battle of Langside of 1568. Mary Queen of Scots army was defeated there, and we researched it for my pathfinder badge. I also made endless cups of tea for family and at local coffee mornings for my Hostess badge.

The overnight trips at Brownie camp were particularly special, the midnight feasts that were probably more around 9pm and the sense of being a part of something. I always really missed my mum when I was away and was so excited to go home and share all my news with her. My mum also helped my sister Christine when she was a Guide leader and I have several memories and photos of her smiling and laughing at being part of the guide group. She also took on a Saturday job with her in Radio Rentals, a TV rental shop in Victoria Road when she was in her late fifties. I would have been about fourteen. She must have been the oldest Saturday girl ever!

My mum had a strong faith in God and it gave her solace, particularly in the latter stages of her life. Her plastic carrier bag she kept at the side of her bed which would always contain multiple prayer cards, novenas and precious relics. They would be brought out every night and you could always rely on my mum to keep you in her prayers or light a candle for you. I too have carried faith, maybe not as much religiously, but certainly spiritually. I believe that one day I will be with her and my dad again. Holding on to this belief continues to provide me with great comfort. This couldn't be the end. My life was only just beginning and theirs had just ended.

*

Eighteen is quite a vulnerable age to lose your parents as you're not technically a child anymore but you're not really an adult either. I had to grow up overnight and I felt cheated. However, despite my grief, I was always aware how blessed I had been having them, even if it was just for a short time. Some people don't even get that, and others never have the happy parent and child relationship which I had.

I am still sad though, at all the events and achievements in my adult life that they haven't been a part of. So many times, I ached for my mum to hold me and tell me like no other can, that it would be all be ok. I often think how fortunate people are to still have their parents around when they are older, in their 30s and 40s, and beyond. For myself, I wish I had the opportunity to have cared for my mum and dad with the knowledge, skills, and wisdom I acquired through my nursing career and life experience.

Perhaps, because she died when I was so young, I always had this image of my mum being perfect. She was so kind, loving and beautiful inside and out. She faced many obstacles, including her inability to have children of her own, as well as my dads' chronic health conditions and her cancer battles. Raising three girls on a tight budget couldn't have been easy and there were times when we probably didn't have much, especially during the time of the strikes but it never felt like that, it always felt like we had enough. My mum made sure of that.

There are stories from my sisters about times where it sounds like my mum was extremely stubborn about certain things or with certain people, namely with siblings or in laws but I don't get defensive now, its ok because she was only human. I am certain that her perception, how she saw the world, was driven from a place of love. We were everything to her and she was fiercely protective of us all. No, my mum wasn't perfect in the eyes of the world, but she definitely was to me.

My mum's birthday was on the 20th of March and Mother's Day sometimes falls around that time. She loved daffodils and tulips and so when I see them now, they always remind me of her and of course it also brings the anticipation of spring. I loved Easter Sunday as a child as it meant getting a new outfit, singing in the choir and of course lots of Easter eggs. Spring has always been my favourite season, bringing its uplifting promise of new life and hope. The time I spent with my mum was short but so precious and I will never forget her love and kindness.

CHAPTER 5

Novice to Nurse

I was accepted for my nurse training in the summer of 1989. The interview was held at the nursing college, based in the Southern General, another large teaching hospital in Govan in the south-west of Glasgow. It's now known as The Queen Elizabeth Hospital. They offered me a place to commence my training the following year and gave me the news that day. I couldn't wait to get home and tell my mum and dad. This was of course in the days before mobile phones, so in the meantime I excitedly told a couple of strangers on the bus ride home. In fact, I think most of the number 34 bus heard me. I was quite literally bursting with pride.

I remained on at school for sixth year and then began my course. My class was divided into around sixty or so student's, half of which did our coursework at the Southern General and the majority of our placements in the Victoria Infirmary, which was fondly called The Viccy. The others remained at the Southern for both. The quote in those days was that the Southern trained nurses and the Viccy trained ladies! I'm not so sure about that. I don't remember any of us being particularly lady-like but we all turned out good nurses! The Viccy sadly closed in 2015 as part of a massive modernisation programme for Glasgow hospitals. It was a friendly hospital and is still greatly missed. I was in one of the last modular classes which consisted of a six-week block in college followed by a three-month placement in the wards and clinical areas over a three-year period. There were eight modules in total. Several different teaching methods have been adopted since then and now all nursing students require to study at university for a degree.

I was extremely fortunate to experience a wide range of specialities including surgical, medical, psychiatry, care of the elderly, district, maternity and operating theatres too. It gave me a taste of everything. Students, especially at senior level were regarded as vital team players. I strode through those hospital automatic doors every day in the Viccy, the clinical smell immediately permeating my nostrils. Now though, I was no longer a visitor. I was an enthusiastic student nurse. It certainly wasn't all work and no play. I partied hard too, and the weekends usually started on a Thursday and finished on a Sunday!

In September 1990, I started Module 1 of my practical training in Ward 5 of the Viccy. This was a surgical module, and it was a male Nightingale ward. A Nightingale ward is a type of ward that is one large space with no subdivisions and usually has a couple of side rooms for higher levels of privacy or for patients who are isolating. Bed capacity differed but there were around twenty-five patients. The Nightingale wards were so beneficial for the nurses, as the patients could be observed more closely. Although, they didn't offer much in the way of privacy or infection control. They were named after the pioneer of modern nursing, Florence Nightingale.

Wearing my new crisp white uniform and cardboard hat with pride, I properly began my nurse training. One stripe on the hat signified being a junior student, with the hope being you would earn your three stripes as a senior student in your third and final year before qualifying as an RGN, a Registered General Nurse. I remember being so eager to get out there and care for the patients. Obviously, the nursing theory was absolutely needed but it was the hands-on care where the real learning took place.

I was nurtured and supported by many staff members there in Ward 5, but it was a very mixed time for me, having lost my dad only weeks previously and returning home to my sick mum every day, all still at eighteen years old. With each passing week she was deteriorating. A week or so after starting in the ward, I walked down from the top area of the ward, wondering why all the curtains were drawn round each of the patients' beds. I suddenly became rooted to the spot, and I felt a real anguish in the pit of my stomach as I saw the porters bringing out a patient in a covered trolley. A patient had died from the ward across the corridor, and it was standard practice to shield the other patients from seeing this.

Despite my grief, I embraced this new chapter, throwing myself into my placement and my studies. One morning sticks particularly in my mind, involving a man in his fifties who had had surgery only a day or so previously for a colostomy. A colostomy is an operation to divert one part of the bowel through an opening on the abdomen. The opening is called a stoma, and a pouch is placed over it to collect the faeces externally. I remember Allan (big Al) the third-year senior student and the enrolled nurse Stewart and I going to check the patients wound. This was the first ever stoma I had seen, and I wasn't really prepared for it, all the redness and swelling surrounding it. I clearly remember the feeling of the room spinning, my mouth dry, like I was going to faint. I instinctively knew though that I couldn't allow the patient to see the affect this had on me. This was my first post operative wound I had ever seen. I managed to hold it together and I hope I was as professional as I could be. It was a surgery that indeed had saved this man's life, but in this case it was non reversible and would no doubt impact his life and body image on an ongoing basis. Even at that early stage I knew surgical wards weren't for me.

There were a few patients who died whilst I was on placement there but mainly, I was looking after patients who were admitted for emergency or planned surgical procedures and who were then discharged home. I saw a lot of death however in my next ward placement for the medical module, Module 2.

A medical ward is for patients who have medical issues, such as diabetes, strokes, cardiac issues etc. I was assigned to Ward 17, the same ward in which my dad had been admitted regularly and where he had died. Some of my nursing friends and colleagues went through their whole training and early staff nurse posts without witnessing a single cardiac arrest or death. Yet, in this particular ward which held such painful memories for me, is where I witnessed the most death. It was also the place where I learnt how to carry out the last offices for someone with dignity and respect and that never left me.

Last offices are the care given to a body after death. It's a process that demonstrates respect for the deceased person and taking into consideration any religious or cultural beliefs that the patient may have had. I always cared for the patients in a way in which I would want and expect my own family to be looked after. It was for me, the last act of kindness and care a nurse can give and I always felt it an honour to be able to do this.

The last time I had seen my dad before he died was in bed six, being right there on a daily basis held mixed emotions for me. Seeing that bed every day was upsetting and yet, at the same time I felt comforted working alongside the people who had cared for him. Sister McLaren was the ward sister and in charge of Ward 17 and she was extremely kind to me, as were so many others. I also felt protected by my dad in some way, especially on nightshifts. This was my first experience of working a nightshift and it was daunting at times, especially with the number of cardiac arrests which occurred.

At that time there were nursing officers in hospitals (their names have since been changed to nursing coordinators which sounds less terrifying) and they were rather strict! They would come to the ward at least once during the nightshift to check with the nurse in charge if everything was ok. Everyone without exception feared them. Every student who did the nightshift rota would be summoned in the early hours of the morning, to stand at the foot of each bed. There was an expectation from the nursing officers for each student to confidently know and be able to provide them with patients' details. This included their name, age, diagnosis and in general how they had been. It was nerve wracking, and I breathed a huge sigh of relief when my turn was over.

It was also a physically demanding job. There were lifting aids to assist in moving the patients but generally they were moved up the bed with nothing but the sheer power of the nursing staff. A favourite way to move bed-bound patients was the Australian lift, a regular practice which involved two nurses placing their shoulders under the patient's armpit to lift them. This practice was subsequently banned as it puts strain on the patients' shoulders and the nurse's back. It was a personal favourite of mine at the time, although maybe my lower back years later, would now disagree!

It's hard to believe that you were allowed in those days to smoke inside the hospital, and this applied to both patients and staff. There was a small room near the changing rooms, beside the hospital canteen, where the staff would congregate on their tea breaks or before starting a shift. On my first ever nightshift I nervously sat and lit a cigarette, unfortunately placing the match back in the box too soon so it set the whole box of matches alight. I started that shift reeking of smoke and I invested in a lighter after that!

What nightshift did make me appreciate more though was toast. A simple but much welcomed pleasure. There was no better smell or taste of it, than when around 5.30 in the morning out would come the tea and toast before the process of starting "the back round." This involved getting the patients wakened and their position changed if required before breakfast. I remember the sheer gratitude of the dayshift relieving you from your overnight jetlag exhaustion.

*

My mum died towards the end of my placement in Ward 17. I often regretted over the years about not taking time off and caring for my own mum instead of looking after other people's parents, but I feel now that my mum wouldn't have wanted that. That took a long time for me to realise and accept through a lot of reflection and counselling in later years. However, through this process I am now gentler and more understanding of my teenage self. I only took two days off as sick leave for both my mum and dad's funerals, but the nurse training rules then were strict. You were only allowed a small amount of sick leave per module. There certainly was no health and wellbeing support from the college to speak of in those days . Given the huge rise in mental health awareness now in the workplace surrounding issues such as dealing with grief, I am sure things have changed for the better. I don't regret what I did, as if I had taken more time off (I felt I had to keep some days up my sleeve in case of illness) then I would have been put back a class and wouldn't have had the precious lifelong friendships I have now, more than 30 years later. Having said this all this, how could I ever have begun to process and grieve with only two days off!

*

I booked my first girls' holiday several months before my mum died. So, less than two weeks after her funeral, I was in Canet Plage in the South of France on a ten-day holiday in a caravan park. It was low season and incredibly quiet but the six of us certainly livened it up. We met a crowd of boys from Cornwall, and we had a ball! I was just a normal teenager desperate for my first holiday abroad with friends but looking back I was probably still in a degree of shock. Despite this, I have such fond memories of that caravan in France, the parties, the laughs and the feeling of belonging in a great crowd. I returned home on a twenty-four-hour coach trip, after constant drinking and smoking, totally exhausted.

Trips to the GP thereafter were standard practice after any of my holidays abroad with the girls. A phone call to my sister Yvonne back in Glasgow a few days before arriving back home to book an appointment. Guaranteed I would have developed a throat or chest infection by then with all the duty-free cigarettes. One thing however I never came back with was a tan. Not just because of my pale celtic skin and freckles but because I never actually saw any sun. We spent all our holidays in the Scottish and Irish bars. We would get back to our accommodation between 7 and 8 o'clock in the morning and then I would sleep all day to recover. I'm so glad we didn't have the pressures of teenagers and young adults now, the scrutiny and social media worries. The call to my sister from a phone box and a couple of disposable cameras were as technical as it got. The anticipation and excitement of the holiday's spools being developed. No filters and the cameras never lied!

The exhaustion didn't leave me however after the France trip and I knew that hangovers didn't last this long. My GP took a variety of blood tests, and they confirmed her suspicion that I had glandular fever. I continued to work throughout the illness, constantly physically and mentally shattered. It was quite debilitating. This lasted quite acutely for around a year. The losses I had endured, only taking a couple of days off for each parent dying plus drinking alcohol and regular shift work were taking their toll. With the knowledge about self-care that I have now, I realise the likelihood is that by not resting properly from the glandular fever or taking time to acknowledge or process my grief, resulted in years of extreme fatigue for me. I regularly fell asleep in class, much to the bemusement of the college lecturers. The feeling of exhaustion would never really leave me until I was in my thirties.

Psychiatry was our next module. I spent six weeks in a Care of the Elderly ward at the Southern General and then six weeks at Levendale Psychiatric Hospital in Crookston in Glasgow.

Unfortunately, I didn't enjoy my Care of the Elderly placement there at all. This was probably partly due to the tiredness I was facing on a daily basis, but mainly because there were very poor standards of nursing care. I didn't feel there was a holistic approach and having been placed previously in two caring and well ran wards, I found this extremely difficult. I didn't feel much kindness and compassion was shown to the patients by many of the staff. I remember the patients all sat round the day room in a circle, all day every day. There was no stimulation for them, other than a television tucked away somewhere where most of them couldn't see. I was grateful that this hadn't been my first placement. It just didn't have a nice feel to it. Most of the students were shocked and disheartened with this placement and on reflection should have formally complained to the Nursing College. Being so young though, a mere junior student and quite frankly just battling constantly with the exhaustion didn't help. I learnt to find my voice after my training however and became an advocate for those who were unable to speak for themselves or were vulnerable. I was lucky to later find that care of the elderly settings could both have high standards and good care.

The positives however from my time in psychiatry were that I formed close friendships with a couple of the other students on placement there, Carolanne and Cheryl, and after this, our friendship groups got together, so again, I saw the gratitude in that unhappy placement.

I spent the next module at Yorkhill hospital, the Children's hospital in Glasgow. This was to be six long weeks, in a rheumatology ward. A lot of the young children there had debilitating arthritic illnesses and were really limited in what they could do. I felt completely out of my depth, and it was difficult at this young age myself to see children struggling with pain or immobility. Some of the trained staff were obviously disinterested with the student nurses. It felt soul destroying travelling there every day. I tried desperately hard to join in conversations at break times but was brazenly ignored. It just seemed that students were nuisances, although I know this wasn't the case in every ward and some friends had incredibly positive experiences. It was also a rather quiet environment, the ward was rarely at full capacity, so nothing much for a student to do. The parents and kids kept me going. For some reason the late shifts were worse, much quieter, so they seemed to drag in more. I spent most nights in tears at the bus stop after the eight-hour long late shifts around 10pm.

CHAPTER 6

Moving On Up

Thankfully, those negative experiences in that phase of my nurse training ended with the next module, as I ventured into the health visiting, district and maternity world. I particularly loved my placements in district and health visiting in Rutherglen Health Centre. I can't remember the names of the nurses I worked with, but I do recall clearly their kindness. It was a remarkably busy practice, but I always felt welcomed and maybe I appreciated this more due to the previous placements. It restored my faith in my training greatly. I loved maternity too and I witnessed seven births in total. The most special one for me was a baby being born to a couple who were in their forties and had struggled with infertility for a long time. I felt honoured and blessed, witnessing their miracle baby making its appearance into the world.

*

In 1992, I entered my senior student days, having coveted three stripes on my hat. I now had senior surgical and medical placements, along with Accident and Emergency, Intensive Care, Coronary Care, Theatres and management blocks. I did enjoy and indeed learn from all these placements, but I knew they weren't for me. I didn't embrace, like others, the adrenaline rush or anticipation of the standby phone ringing in Accident and Emergency. This informed the team of any traumatic injuries or disasters coming in. If any of the students were asked if they wanted to observe these, I would politely decline and luckily for me there was always another student who would be keen. That was the great advantage about our training, the diversity, and the exposure to different types of specialities with different paces.

But of course, it wasn't just the training and gaining knowledge I loved, it was the social life it brought. Singing in the Karaoke nights in the pubs in Battlefield and Shawlands and in the famous Horseshoe bar in Glasgow. The Horseshoe is still well renowned for folk belting out a tune. Tammy Wynette's "Stand by your man" and "D.I.V.O.R.C.E" were my go-to songs, with a wee bit of Madonna thrown in sometimes! Those times of fun, dancing and singing allowed me to be just like everyone else, not Catriona who had lost both parents, who felt a huge amount of shouldering other's pain and sorrow as a nurse. Music and dance allowed me to forget the responsibility. It gave me a sense of freedom and joy and it's something which I started to embrace again, albeit with the radio on in the kitchen mostly.

As nursing students, we all came from different backgrounds, from as far afield as Skye or a stone's throw away, like me in Victoria Road but we all shared something in common, our desire to care and be good nurses. We had a thirst for knowledge as well as alcohol and our friendships helped get us through our training. Apart from myself, all my class of August 1990 friends still remain in nursing or midwifery. Although we don't get the chance to meet up as often as we would like due to family or work commitments or living on the other side of the world in Australia, it doesn't really matter because we are bound together with a deep love and respect for each other. We laugh, cry and have continued to be be there for each other individually and collectively through painful and traumatic times. We witnessed so much through our professional and personal lives, and I am forever grateful for their friendship and love as I know they are off mine.

By far, it was the wards and medical modules I enjoyed the most. I loved everything about them, the variety of medical conditions the patients had, the hectic pace, no two days were ever the same. I loved the hands-on nursing care and the feeling of making a difference to patients and for their families. This was a vocation for me and there was no doubt in my mind that my dad had been right when he had said many times that I was born for this .

CHAPTER 7

Things Can Only Get Better

When I completed my training in October 1993, I applied for a job in a nursing home in Glasgow and was successful. I remember though, the negative reaction from many people when I told them. The most common was *"Oh could you not get anything else?"* but although that surprised me at the time, it doesn't now. I love elderly people and I think the way we look at elderly care and the individuals providing it should be regarded with more respect and financial input.

Darnley Court Nursing Home was a brand-new home with four units, two general and two psychiatric and it was exciting to be part of a fresh team starting out. Most of the staff nurses were newly qualified like me or with little experience. We were placed initially in Cowglen Hospital, a care of the elderly hospital nearby. I was there for a few weeks prior to the nursing home opening as most of the patients were to come from there. Thankfully I was only in Cowglen for a few weeks as literally within days of being a newly qualified nurse, it was decided I would need to take charge on the nightshift on Christmas Eve. It proved to be the longest night of my life, there was no other trained nurse on. It was just myself and a couple of auxiliary nurses from another ward, but they were so kind and helpful to me. It took me about three hours to give the medications out, then a patient fell out of the bed onto a radiator without a cover on it, sustaining a burn to his face. I contacted the on-call Doctor who gave me a rollicking as it was about 11.30 pm and I had misread the rota and had called him by mistake. This would not be the first strained conversation I would have with this man during my post there. Fortunately, the GP that came out that night was kind and understanding. I can't remember much else about that night other than I was like a rabbit caught in headlights. Every nurse will remember their first shift they were placed in charge. I was never so glad to get home that morning and to finish my time in Cowglen.

Our transfer, however, to the nursing home was a new and exciting chapter. We had the most wonderful sister, Karen McGregor who epitomised to me what a nurse and sister should be. She was so caring and compassionate and a great team player too. She taught me so much and I learnt a lot of skills there. Beaton ward where I was placed was a thirty bedded unit with single rooms. It was hard work but there was a warmth and a camaraderie amongst the staff and love for the residents which shone through and made the long shifts rewarding and worthwhile. There was entertainment, good food, and the families and residents became like your own.

During the covid pandemic when all those vulnerable people died in care homes, my heart went out to those who lost their lives and for the staff looking after them. Some people can be there for years, and you can develop such a strong bond with them. There can be a lot of criticism and bad press about nursing homes but mine was a positive and rewarding experience. I loved hearing all about the residents' pasts and over thirty years later I can still remember individuals' names and their stories. With covid, we saw the sacrifice that many carers and staff up and down the country had made to protect our elderly and most vulnerable in society. The devastation of spouses, children and other family members not seeing their loved ones was unimaginable for me and so real for them. Garden visits and window visits were granted eventually but I can only imagine the distress for relatives and patients who could not be physically together towards the end of their lives during lockdown. To sit and comfort, to just be there. It can't be underestimated either the impact that the pandemic has had on the nurses, doctors, and the healthcare workers, anyone who works in hospital, community and social care, and the distress it must have caused. I wonder how I would have coped with all that in the nursing home aged twenty-two, especially after losing my own mum and dad only a few years previously.

*

I was still extremely tired in the nursing home, and then I began to experience nausea on a daily basis. This was investigated with blood tests and scans, but nothing appeared to be medically wrong. The feeling of sickness eventually subsided after six months or so. After eighteen months there, I decided I wanted a change and having loved my medical placements as a student nurse, I applied for one of several staff nurse posts at the Viccy. It also had the bonus of being a ten-minute walk away, cutting out the two-hour commute on the bus each day. I was successful and was asked to start a month later. I was initially meant to start in Ward 15, but I got a phone call several days later, to say it would be Ward 17 instead! I couldn't seem to get away from this place. I remember being quite reluctant, it was five years now since my lovely Dad had died there. As much as I had loved my student nurse times, I honestly wondered if I could cope in that particular ward, after all that I had been through.

CHAPTER 8

Ward 17

Ward 17 of the Viccy was a general male medical ward. The patients were admitted with a range of chronic or acute conditions, mainly with respiratory disease, diabetes, stroke and liver disease. The men who developed liver disease mostly, but not always, as a result of alcohol dependence. Working with men with alcohol addictions was common in Ward 17. You witnessed first-hand the devastation that alcohol can cause both to the individual and their families. It never mattered to me or indeed I believe most of the staff, what the reason for admission was. Whether it was the twenty-seven-year-old who felt that if he didn't have alcohol then he had nothing to live for, or the men who held down full-time responsible jobs. As far as we were concerned, they were all in our care and should be treated equally. The nursing staff worked closely with the gastroenterology staff and Dr Forrest from that team was such an inspiring consultant to me, an extremely compassionate man. It was a pleasure to work alongside him during his time there. He taught us all so much and he looked after his patients with kindness.

I spent eight years in Ward 17 in total. After six years, aged twenty-eight I applied for the ward sister's post. My only hesitation for applying was the concern that I wouldn't be as much hands-on with the patients and lose that part of what was essentially being a nurse for me, carrying out nursing care. I was so passionate about that ward, the patients and the staff. I never had any real concern though, that I would change or would have to. I believed I could make a real difference just the way I was, as a ward sister. I may have been young but had a lot of life experience. Added to this, I had acted up in the role for six months or so whilst Ruth the ward sister at that time was on a secondment, so I knew the responsibility and hard work that lay ahead.

When I applied for the post, I was aware that whilst I was experienced and capable of running a hectic and busy ward, I didn't have a nursing degree. Others applying did or were in the process of doing so, so I said on my application form that I was planning to start. So, after being successful, I reckoned I had to keep my promise.

I started a four-year part-time University degree at Caledonia university in Glasgow. This was challenging, finding the time to study and work full time, especially as time management was never my strongest point. I was also extremely tired and lacking in energy at times. I still, however, was managing a busy social life and burning the candle at both ends! I remember in particular my friend and colleague Lynne helping me complete several assignments. She stayed up with me until 2am on the day one of my essays was due in, encouraging and motivating me, despite the fact we had both just done a busy late shift and were up again at 6am for work.

Wearing my navy-blue sister's uniform was definitely my armour. For someone who struggled somewhat to stand up for herself in many ways, when it came to my patients, I always had courage. I'm sure it was because I always felt my dad was beside me, encouraging me and keeping me safe from the violent confrontations with patients that I often faced. I treated my staff with respect and in turn they did me. It was like riding a rollercoaster there most days. I continuously found myself being an advocate for those who otherwise wouldn't have had a voice. Although sometimes, it was difficult for my wee self to stand up to some individuals, (mainly Consultants) I always did if I genuinely believed something was in the best interest of the patient. I wouldn't hold back.

Ward 17 was a legendary ward- if you could work there, you could quite literally work anywhere.

Nursing doesn't just require care and compassion; it requires a sense of humour and an ability to multitask. You certainly needed these attributes in abundance to work there. Over the course of my nursing career, I found that if you have a good team behind you, then you can work in any challenging and stressful environments.

Winning an NHS award in 2000 for outstanding nursing care was such a fantastic achievement for the whole team and I was so proud. It was enough for the team to be nominated, never mind winning! I was presented our award that night from the Mayor of Glasgow at the City Chambers at a lovely ceremony alongside Marjorie and Norma, two of the night shift auxiliaries. Both Marjorie and Norma were fantastic nurses and good friends. I beamed from ear to ear that night and the pride I felt was like that day back in 1989 when I had been accepted into nursing, and later when I got my Ward Sisters post.

We had so many nights out and good times, but one of my favourite ones had to be the talent show. It was a one-off event one Christmas time, and all the acts raised the roof! It was held in the lecture theatre at the Viccy. There was a variety of acts from different departments but the two I remember most were (obviously) our act and Dr Shouren Datta's. A group of staff from our ward danced to Grease Lightening; we practiced lots in my flat in Viccy Road in preparation for it and literally laughed till we cried. It was one of the most fun things I have ever done, and I loved being on stage. Shouren was Robbie Williams; he sang and danced his heart out to "Let Me Entertain you". I can still picture him, appearing from the top of the steps in the room, bursting into song in his Robbie costume. The atmosphere was electric, and the Ward 17 crew were giddy with excitement (and alcohol) I'm not sure who won the show in the end, but it didn't matter, we all had a blast. Happy days!

*

I believe I possessed strong leadership skills and I appreciated and nurtured my colleagues. Having someone who motivates and guides their staff proves beneficial to the atmosphere and ethos of the ward or environment, which in turn positively affects patient care. I was fortunate on so many levels to have many influential and caring mentors. There were some who weren't so good, but that's the way of life, and you learn from both. What I did learn early on was how important the auxiliary nurses were and how they played a fundamental role in the team.

However overall, the people I probably learnt from the most were the patients themselves, their stories and their experiences. They placed their trust in you and for the majority of the time they were incredibly grateful. I witnessed people at their most vulnerable. As a nurse you have a ringside seat on some of the most intimate parts of people's lives, their illnesses and the impact this has on them and their loved ones.

There were many incidents over the years where we had to persuade men who absconded from the wards in a confused state to return. Not an easy task, and it became a regular occurrence to chase big strapping men down the fire escape or through the streets of Battlefield, usually as a result of the DTs - Delirium tremens. DTs are a severe form of alcohol withdrawal and can cause confusion, aggression and hallucinations. It generally involved the porters and police in assisting us with escorting them back to the ward. The porters were invaluable, they helped you out so much in situations which were I am sure felt dangerous and scary for them, but it always felt they had our backs. We may have been short staffed at times, but the support was like an army behind you. I recall one of many incidents, I was finishing my early shift, around four in the afternoon, (my usual hour later than I should have finished) and normally changed out of my uniform but this particular time I kept it on to return home. I just felt uneasy about one of the patients who had alcohol issues. He was becoming increasingly agitated over the course of the day and hadn't been prescribed the adequate dose of Librium (which is used for alcohol withdrawal) I just had that instinct, my vibes that things weren't right, that he was going to get worse. Despite my pleas to the medical staff, his medication wasn't increased, however I do know that patients are not completely truthful at times with their alcohol consumption intake. This would have inevitably played a part in what happened next. I went home but couldn't really settle, so I called the staff to see how he was after a couple of hours. All hell had broken loose, he had assaulted several members of staff and was currently being restrained by the police and was given an intramuscular injection to sedate him. I returned immediately and found the patients and staff extremely shaken and some tearful. It had been a terrifying experience. I had to cancel the evenings visiting times. I remember walking out in the corridor to inform the relatives and there were some unhappy people but in general they were very understanding.

Another time on nightshift we had an escapee who was then found later, brought to Accident and Emergency and was being extremely violent from the DTs. He had been sedated there and we were to take him back. He was to go into bed 5 right at the nurse's station where we could observe him. Generally, the sickest or the most confused patients were beside the nurse's station area for observational purposes. The consultant Mr Anderson came through the doors, with several male staff and porters. The double doors were parted, and it felt like the cavalry bringing him back. Back to four female staff responsible for twenty-five patients! We watched him like a hawk, and we didn't hear a peep out of him thankfully. He discharged himself the next day.

I had many experiences over the years that I spent in ward 17 that were tough, but towards the end of my time there I had an extremely traumatic shift. A young man was transferred to us from a psychiatric hospital as he had medical issues as well as psychiatric. He attempted to take his own life on the ward but fortunately I got there on time. A lack of support that night from the senior doctor on call and the stress of having to call this young man's mum to inform her of the events was very distressing for me. We had the minimal staff on, this young man was strong and quite obviously acutely mentally ill and I was fearful for his life. I stayed for hours after my shift ended that night, I was terrified that he would try to take his life again. The night shift co Ordinator Anne McGuiness was supportive and persuaded me to go home, as it was, by this time after midnight and my shift had ended two hours previously. I came onto my next shift about six hours later to thankfully find two psychiatric nurses beside him. I hadn't slept much, if at all and I was on autopilot. I was in a daze that day, and probably shouldn't have remained on duty, despite the pleas from my manager and staff to go home. I got an urgent occupational health appointment that day which really helped. I really felt supported, and I appreciated the opportunity to speak about that event, which I have no doubt helped me in not suffering any long-term effects from this experience. Thankfully the young man was transferred back to a psychiatric setting the following day.

There were many more challenging times in Ward 17 but being part of a fantastic team helped immensely. I loved working there; the buzz of the place and the shifts were always so busy. However, there were also some truly awful moments with violence and sadness when patients died. There was frustration and anger sometimes at the out-of-date facilities which rose to the surface in medical emergency situations. The ward was sub divided into bed bays of four patients or bays with two patients, which made it difficult to observe anyone who was extremely ill. There were only eight oxygen points in the main ward for twenty-one males until its eventual refurbishment in 1999. It was a huge undertaking, and we were chosen as the first ward in the Viccy to undergo these vast improvements.

The new ward became a nightingale ward, which from an observation perspective was going to be so much better. We were all really excited about our new environment, oxygen points and suction points at every bed now. No more lassoing suction and oxygen tubing across bed bays in emergency situations. There was a reduction in bed numbers and a lot to be excited about, but I was starting to struggle with my mental health. I wasn't sleeping well and was worrying about a lot of things in general. Thoughts of how it would all go, the extra workload of packing everything up and the detailed coordination required to move extremely sick patients to another ward was taking its toll on me. Not only that, but we were also moving (albeit temporarily) to another antiquated ward with similar outdated features. We had to move everything, unpack and reopen our brand-new shiny ward late November time in 2001. Despite a few hiccups initially, i.e. pipes bursting at 2am on a nightshift and items falling off walls, it was a safer and better environment to work in and care for patients. We could see the patients properly now. I had made my feelings known for years regarding the levels of violence we experienced and the safety concerns for the staff. An emergency button was installed in the ward that we were able to press which gave us direct access for police assistance if required. It certainly made the team feel more secure.

At that point, I felt like my colleagues, and I were like a family. We had a great social life, respect for each other and I had the privilege of leading that team. I was young, free and single (after a long-term relationship had ended), was at a great stage in my career, but I was also sad a great deal of the time too. I worked an early shift on Christmas day after the refurbishment was complete. It was unusually quiet, we made the day as nice as possible for the patients, then I went into the duty room and just cried. I felt incredibly sad and lonely, despite being surrounded by people. This was something I seemed to be doing more and more of. I went to my GP shortly after this and was prescribed antidepressants which I stayed on for a year which really helped. The medication was obviously needed but looking back several years later, it probably wasn't enough on its own. I wasn't dealing with my underlying issues of grief, and I hadn't allowed myself the time or space to heal.

CHAPTER 9
The Power of Love

In December 2003, I was asked by management to transfer to Ward 15 to be their ward sister. I was devastated at leaving my second home. This was also a busy medical ward which specialised in looking after patients with respiratory and diabetic issues. There were many palliative care patients with lung cancer and end stage respiratory disease.

Many challenges awaited me in my role there, a whole new team for me to get used to and vice versa, and yet another stressful and exhausting ward decant and refurbishment. There were also regular shifts on the hospital Co- Ordinator rota (which all of the ward sisters/charge nurses in the hospital did), but there were so many positives too. I worked with many caring and lovely staff, some of whom just needed a bit of confidence and self-belief, which I was able to help them with.

Of course, the best thing about working there was because it was the ward in which I met Graham, my future husband. My first impressions of Graham were that he was an extremely kind and calm doctor. I only ever met him briefly before in

Ward 17 when he was on call and reviewed patients. He radiated warmth and comfort to his patients and their families. Our love story wasn't so much love at first sight, but rather, a slow burner. I began to work with him daily. He was the SHO, a position known then as a Senior House Officer. He always held the same, gentle and compassionate tone with patients. He was well liked and respected by his patients. It was during his time there that he decided to embark on a career in palliative medicine. A few months after we started working together, I realised that my feelings had developed from just being a work colleague into something deeper- but it took a while for the penny to drop with the big G!

I started to organise some nights out with Alan, the other SHO who became a great friend. I held a big party at mine one night and the rest as they say is history. My regular parties instigated several Viccy romances, some of which also led to marriage, including ours.

The first six months for Graham and I involved lots of dinner dates and nights at the pub. For the first time since I lost my parents all those years ago, I felt protected and loved. I didn't feel lonely anymore. There's no doubt that this loving and nurturing relationship triggered and then allowed the trauma and grief I had held onto to come to the surface. Meeting Graham would allow me to feel in a safe place without judgement to grieve and acknowledge the losses and pain that had weighed so heavily on my shoulders. Graham also was a great sport, and the Ward 15 staff managed to persuade him to dress up as Santa Claus on Christmas Day, parading him along the ward, on top of the tea trolley, ringing the bell we used to use to chuck relatives (or should I say encourage them) to leave after visiting time. Graham was and still is my rock throughout the time we've been together.

I looked after many men in both Ward 15 and 17, for whom this would be their last admission. They died in these busy and sometimes hectic places. I sat with the young and the old, and never forgot that this was a privileged part of my job, to be with someone in their final weeks, days and moments. Then, I guided their families and loved ones gently back to a quiet space, after they had said their goodbyes. Compassionately listening, whilst also providing information on practical issues such as registering their loved one's death. Some would weep, be angry or appear in a state of shock particularly if the death had been sudden. I always knew how important this part of my role was. I had no second chances to get this right. I tried to make families feel that they and their loved ones were the most important people at that time and give them the time they needed to ask questions or just release their emotions. This is how I had been made to feel by Sister Ruby at the hospice at on my mum's final day there which made me endeavour to do the same.

There are many patients and situations I remember, but one that only recently came to mind was when I was a staff nurse in Ward 17, a couple of years after I started. We had several extremely ill patients and three died within a period of ten minutes. That was extremely rare, but it had a real impact on me. I just froze, reminiscent of that day in ward 5 when I saw the porters bringing out the patient. I knew I couldn't do it, not that day, I couldn't cope with carrying out the last offices and comforting relatives. It was decided that I would move to another medical ward for a couple of hours which was relatively quiet. This was yet another example of getting on with it, but on reflection another experience that was taking its toll on my body and mind.

Death and trauma are things that most of the nursing and healthcare professionals are exposed to. It shouldn't mean that we just expect them to cope with it and we must not underestimate the effects it can have. We need to nurture our NHS and care workers, many who are suffering from burnout and compassion fatigue, especially after the past few years.

I still remember clearly how that day affected me, so I can't even begin to imagine the impact on the staff in areas that lost so many patients with Covid on a daily basis.

So many lives are saved with medicine and expert care from doctors, surgeons and nursing staff. However, I have no doubt that the love and devotion from family members can be just as imperative. One remarkable woman stands out to me. James's wife came to every single visit after her husband was admitted to Ward 17 with a devastating stroke. Initially he had a tracheostomy (an opening created at the front of the neck where a tube is inserted into the trachea (windpipe) to allow patients to breathe) The tracheostomy itself requires a lot of care and attention which proved challenging in such a busy environment. His wife sat daily at his bedside, talking to him and encouraging him, and against all odds, he gradually improved, despite pneumonias and other complications. James and his wife were both in their seventies and she herself had some health issues. Miraculously, James was able to eventually improve enough to eat, transfer from bed to chair and go home to be with his devoted wife with a care package after a period in a rehabilitation ward. We were all amazed at the progress he had made and the obstacles he had overcome but I had no doubt that the love and devotion shown by his wife was a big part of his recovery, along with his own determination.

In Ward 15 I nursed a man in his fifties with a chronic illness who required a lot of nursing care. He had been cared for at home by his wife who was his primary carer. A few of the staff had mentioned that his wife was being demanding and critical, but she had been with him day in day out caring for him. I arranged a chat with her and asked if she would like to come in out- with visiting hours so she could assist him in mealtimes and with aspects of hygiene etc. I know this would not be feasible for every patient but sometimes it can be the right thing to do. No more seemingly demanding conversations took place after that.

People need to feel heard and just allowing her to talk and be involved in her husbands' care was so important for them both. It taught me that these patients were not mine. They were in hospital to be cared for, in my care, but they were individuals with their own choices and different needs and sometimes we didn't always know best.

In my last year or so of nursing in Ward 15, we had two patients who were with us for around six months. Their beds were the first you saw as you entered the ward. Despite having devastating diagnoses, they both had a great sense of humour and always happy to see you. Both were young- in their sixties. When Edward died it was an incredibly sad day, his wife had visited every day, and we got to know the family well. His death was felt not only by the staff, but by Henry whose bed was next to Edwards. They had been such great companions to each other. Henry was, a short time later, discharged to a nursing home.

*

Although it's important to be professional, its ok too to express your own emotions and not bottle things up, particularly in areas where death is common. We didn't have reflection as such, but we did as a team in both wards support each other. I wore my heart on my sleeve, and I did cry often, sometimes with sadness at losing a patient. Other times, out of sheer frustration at out-of-date facilities or a feeling of not being able to provide the high standard of care I had wanted. Then I would be embarrassed for allowing these emotions in the workplace. Sadly, some people see expressing grief in their professional role, as a sign of weakness, whereas I have come to learn that it can be the opposite and actually a strength.

I'm not naive however and I know not all deaths were as peaceful as hoped for, or that all families were happy with the care that their loved one had received. However, as an individual and collectively as a team, we always strived to do our best.

I know that having experienced loss at an early age with my grandparents, then my parents, and growing up where illness and hospital visits were a part of our lives, plus all the death I was exposed to as a nurse has made me love life and I have a greater appreciation for it.

My desire to care for people, in illness and in their final days was all I ever wanted to do, but I had not really acknowledged or taken the time to listen to what my own body was telling me. My inner voice was pleading with me to slow down and take time out. There was a lot of guilt associated with not caring for my Mum, sadness at my losses plus the tremendous sense of duty and responsibility I felt for other people's grief. No one else made me feel like this, this was me. The load was becoming heavier and heavier.

CHAPTER 10

The Relative Incident

In late September 2004, I endured an extremely upsetting incident with a relative of a patient. This was the catalyst to my breakdown or, as I now call it, my breakthrough.

One Saturday night after visiting hours, a very irate patient's son and his wife wanted to speak with me about their dad. He was dying of lung cancer. I understood their fear and anxiety at the prospect of losing him, from both a personal and professional perspective, but no-one should be subjected to the level of verbal abuse I received. At this point in my career, I was an extremely experienced nurse and regularly dealt with many fraught and challenging individuals. This time however was entirely different. I spent nearly an hour with the son shouting at me unrelentingly. Even my level of empathy had reached its limits. He accused me of being uncaring, and being a terrible ward sister, who didn't know what was going on in her own ward. It was a deeply personal attack which left me shaken to the core.

I can't recall the exact details of that night in terms of all the words that were used. Perhaps this is my coping strategy for this harrowing incident, but I can still remember vividly how it made me feel.

Despite my best efforts to diffuse the situation and answer his concerns, the patient's son continued to aggressively shout. I realised we weren't going to make any progress and I was trying desperately to hold myself together, to be professional. This unacceptable behaviour forced me to do something which I had never done throughout my nursing career. My voice trembled and tears stung my eyes. I knew the floodgates were about to open, so I told them to leave. What I found most distressing was how he appeared to almost enjoy seeing me struggle, with no remorse. At least, that's what it felt like at the time.

I shut the door, and there, in the longest hour of my nursing career, all my years of hard work, believing I was striving to do my best, it all just fell apart. I felt so helpless and personally attacked. I believed nursing was a vocation for me. I wasn't perfect, I'm sure I got things wrong at times, but I went in every day, as I'm sure most nursing and healthcare workers do, to care for people and their loved ones as best I could.

I finished my shift and walked home in a daze. By the time I got into my flat, my chest was aching with heavy sobs. I curled up in a ball in my bed, where I stayed crying for hours. A fitful sleep ensued and then it was back to the ward the following morning.

I'm not suggesting that families don't have the right to express an opinion or ask questions, especially if there are care concerns that need to be addressed, but when staff are trying their level best day in and out, it is crushing. Nurses must remember that a patient or relatives' reaction to something is real to them, and they should feel listened too but equally the nurse has feelings and emotions too which should be respected. In spite of being subjected to this awful tirade by his son, his dad (the patient) was happy with his care. He often thanked us and told us what a good job we were doing, so I held onto that. I never mentioned to him about the conversation, as he was always so grateful, but I really felt a complete failure after this incident.

The patient died about a week later, comfortable and surrounded by his family but his son could not actually look me in the eye, and I could sense his anger towards me. My colleagues were sympathetic, but all probably relieved that it had not been them in the firing line. After all the traumatic things I had witnessed, the deaths and violence and stress, this had the most profound effect on me in my career.

Despite this, I am aware that this was only one incident in an eighteen-year career which in general rewarded me. I can accept that if it hadn't been this relative incident, then it would have been something else that would have brought me to a halt. I only ever told Graham at the time how bad that night made me feel. I was tired, I was sad, and I was completely burnt-out.

It's remarkable how certain events can have such a profound impact, even decades later. Its testament to the depth of our emotions and the significance of our experiences.

CHAPTER 11

Needing Help

A week or so later, my friends and I went for a coffee after work (which inevitably ended up as a bottle of wine) at the Church on the Hill. This wasn't a place of worship but a pub and a regular haunt for Viccy staff at the Battlefield monument. I had a great night, but I became really drunk and as often can be the case with alcohol, the merriness turned to sadness and melancholy, which spiralled into total anguish.

After only a few hours of broken sleep, I went to work the following day, feeling exceptionally hungover. I couldn't seem to eat much, and I felt very nauseous. On top of all this, I ended up being the hospital coordinator that night. A scary enough role at the best of times -dealing with situations ranging from staff absences to cardiac arrests or having to close the hospital to emergency admissions. Stressful enough, without the fear after the drink.

Thankfully though, I had a quiet and uneventful shift, but in spite of this I became more and more tense and anxious as the evening went on. By the time, I handed over the hospital pager and transfer details to the nightshift Coordinator I was shaking. I became restless, and I was trying desperately not to show this which made the symptoms worse. The way I felt that night was nothing like I had ever experienced. I was so agitated but at the same time I was exhausted too. I knew this wasn't just a hangover! I stayed at Grahams flat that night, I went to bed but couldn't lie down. It was incredibly scary, and I didn't know how to describe this hyper alert way I felt to Graham. I had to keep getting up from the bed and sit on a chair and then pace about. There was a feeling of impending doom and a fear of what was happening to me.

After that night I experienced similar episodes regularly and acutely, without consuming alcohol. I tried to sleep with little success, and I couldn't eat much due to feeling so nauseas. I was suffering with dizzy spells and the only way I could stop them was to lie down but when I lay down, I couldn't be still and that would provoke the agitated feeling. It was a never-ending cycle. I made an appointment to see the GP who prescribed an anti- sickness and anti-acid medication which didn't particularly make any difference to my symptoms. I continued at work, still not understanding my physical issues. I was too scared to admit to anyone how I was really feeling apart from Graham. For the first time in my life, I felt my body and mind were out of control.

In December 2004, two months after the incident with the relative, Graham and I travelled to London to stay with friends. I had a panic attack standing in the airport queue. I couldn't breathe.

Where was the air?

What was happening to me?

For anyone who has ever experienced this, it's really frightening. I somehow managed to get on the plane and calmed down with Grahams help and reassurance. I got through that weekend (just) but was completely on edge the whole time. I went to work on the Monday after. Even now, I remember that day so clearly. I walked into the ward for my late- shift, Millie, the Senior staff nurse said "hello" and I just froze. Nothing happened, no one said anything to trigger an emotional response, but I just knew I couldn't do this anymore. I felt so vulnerable and scared, and I just broke down, I was inconsolable. The hospital coordinator came to the ward to see me, and she was so kind and compassionate. It all came tumbling out, how anxious, sad and grief stricken I had been, shouldering the responsibility and burden of other's grief, while I could barely acknowledge my own. I was sent home, and I made an appointment to see the GP a few days later.

I knew I needed to get some professional help. This time I was prescribed a beta blocker called propranolol and told that I was suffering from extreme anxiety. The GP firmly believed that my issues stemmed from psychological factors.

Years previously in the nursing home, when the investigations I underwent for nausea established no abnormalities, the consultant had documented then, that the likelihood was that my symptoms were related to stress. This had never been communicated to me and perhaps if it had, I may have had a better insight into the mind and body connection earlier. Perhaps it's better to ask, *"What has happened to you?" rather than "What's wrong with you?"*

She also offered me antidepressants, but I declined them. I was aware, that at the core of why I felt like this was because of deep seated grief and sadness which I needed to address. It was time to get counselling. I just felt burdened with everything. Two close friends had gently suggested over the years about counselling, but I hadn't sought help. All I knew at this point though was that I didn't want to feel like this anymore. When I came out of the GP surgery that day, I was exhausted but relieved. I felt really listened too and for the first time in several months, I felt there was hope that I could get better. It was like I was carrying the weight of the world on my shoulders. I also had a meeting with my manager, Margaret Arnott, that day; she could see how physically and emotionally drained I was. She insisted I take some time off and rest and her empathy and support are something I've never forgotten.

I felt quite ashamed though of the whole thing. The idea that I could be anxious and need time off. I felt a failure in many ways, that I was struggling, not just with the job I loved, but with daily life. Nowadays, it's relatively common unfortunately for people to be signed off work with stress or anxiety but back then, not so much. Well at least that was my perception at the time.

*

Anxiety is a feeling of unease, a worry or fear which can range from mild to severe. Having anxious thoughts or periods in our lives are normal, such as sitting exams, job interviews or moving home etc, but it can become an issue for many (like me) when it seriously starts to impact daily life. It can be extremely distressing for people as I experienced it, a feeling of constantly being on high alert. At these times a thought or making a simple decision becomes overwhelming and can escalate to a catastrophe. Whilst you are in such a state you continue to be mentally and physically exhausted.

CHAPTER 12

SAD

I took a few weeks off work and made the connection that my low mood also had a definite seasonal element to it. I knew a friend who had SAD, Seasonal Affective Disorder, and the impact this had on her life. I reflected on how I had been since the autumn and winter of my first staff nurse post all those years ago, in the months from October till March. My episodes of depression and anxiety happened in the winter months also. During my sick time, I just slept and cried, frightened of how this anxiety was making me feel. At the time I thought that it had all come out of the blue, but the reality was it had slowly been creeping up on me for over a decade. I decided there and then that my lifestyle had to change. I needed help but I also had to take responsibility (gently) for my emotional and physical wellbeing. I purchased a lightbox (as it is recognised in helping with SAD), and gave up smoking, no patches or nicotine gum. I had tried many times and failed, but not this time.

SAD is a type of depression that comes and goes in a seasonal pattern. The exact cause is not fully understood but it can be linked to the decreased exposure to sunlight in the shorter autumn and winter months. The main theory according to www.nhs.uk is that a lack of sunlight may stop a part of the brain called the hypothalamus working properly, which in turn can affect the production of melatonin, serotonin and your bodies internal clock (circadian rhythm). Melatonin is a hormone that makes you feel sleepy and in people with SAD, the body may produce higher levels. Serotonin is a hormone that affects your mood, appetite and sleep and those who suffer from SAD can produce lower levels during the darker months of the year. This can then lead to really crave carbohydrates which in my case led to weight gain every winter. Lower levels of serotonin caused by a lack of sunlight can also be linked to depression. However, some people with SAD have symptoms in the summer months and feel better during the winter.

My own sadness descended on me gradually like a cloud around October and I always felt my grief intensified throughout these winter months. I didn't understand it at the time. It wasn't that I didn't miss my mum and dad throughout the rest of the year, but it was more acutely felt in the darker nights and mornings. There was an exhaustion, a sense of not wanting to go out. Closing the curtains, blocking out the outside world and a continuous desire to sleep. I now understand the impact that the glandular fever had on me at a young age, coupled with my huge personal losses. Add into this mix, years of demanding shift work and the negative effects that alcohol had on my body along with how the seasons affected me. It was no wonder that, even when things on paper looked good, my job, social life, friends and family, I still felt an overwhelming feeling of sadness.

CHAPTER 13

Sometimes You Can't Make it on Your Own

I desperately wanted to be well and be free of the burden I was carrying. I began my counselling that January and the counsellor was kind, compassionate and she listened without judgement. I had been placed on a waiting list but felt I couldn't wait, so I found a private counsellor, recommended by the GP, something which I appreciate not everyone is able to do. She helped me unravel and work through piece by piece all the years of grief and guilt and anger and loss that I had suffered. I quickly realised that counselling is not for the faint hearted. Initially I went weekly, then fortnightly and then monthly. The sessions were extremely painful, I was constantly being put through an emotional wringer. Every single session, Graham drove me there and waited. We spent our journeys home in silence or with me in floods of tears.

I returned to work around the same time as beginning the counselling, on hindsight maybe not the best idea. However, at least it wasn't back to the wards, shift work and managing nearly thirty staff! I was offered a six-month secondment, setting up a discharge lounge. This was a brand-new area next to the Accident and Emergency Department which provided a space for patients who were being discharged home or to other hospitals to free up beds in the wards. Again, like everything challenges were part and parcel of a senior role and initiating change for some didn't come easy. I was grateful though for the opportunity and it was a lot less demanding. I spent it though, especially on a Wednesday, extremely exhausted after my counselling the night before. I never knew until I experienced it for myself, how tiring it would be. I was weary after all the crying and then putting the brave face on to go to work, the mask!

Perhaps that's why people don't seek help because they are frightened of reliving their traumas or grief. While I do believe in moving forward, until I acknowledged and dealt with certain things, I felt unable to. Counselling is an exhausting process, I would say to anyone who is going through it to be kind to yourself, surround yourself as best you can with supportive and understanding people. It can take a lot of courage for an individual to be open and express how they feel, and a good counsellor is invaluable.

Verbalising our thoughts out loud can be therapeutic. Holding onto guilt, worry and stress can manifest in physical illness and psychological distress. A lot of the time we live in our mind. A worry or a fear of something, (which hasn't happened) starts off small but can quickly spiral into a disaster the more we think about it. Talking it over with a friend or professional can help. Counselling not only helped me acknowledge my feelings from the past but helped me during many life changing and important events that took place during the period of time I was there. One of which was selling the home that I had grown up in, my family home in Victoria Road. This was one of the hardest and best things I have ever done.

CHAPTER 14

New Beginnings

After our mum and dad died, myself, Yvonne and my niece Laura all stayed on in the family home. Christine was married and living not far from us, but I missed her very much. I didn't appreciate at the time how stressful and awful this must have been for her, organising both funerals and all this within the first year of married life. As the oldest sister, she took on this role, she did so much for us then and throughout the years and she knows how much we all love her. She was then diagnosed with thyroid cancer in 1997 and I was terrified I was going to lose her too, but she thankfully made a full recovery. I remember going to visit her on the day of her discharge from the Viccy after her surgery, it was the same day that Princess Diana died, Sunday 31st August 1997. I was so relieved and grateful that she was getting home. Yvonne and Laura moved out in October 1994, and I stayed in the family home for a further twelve years.

Putting the house on the market and getting it ready for sale was painful and emotional. I felt vulnerable, as if my heart was breaking, it was an exhausting process but at the same time I knew in my gut, that I was doing the right thing. Not facing up to things in my life had been a pattern for me. I left my mum and dads bedroom untouched for years and years before I had the strength to go in it, never mind through things. I had also begun a relationship with someone, very soon after my mum died. Despite feeling unhappy and lonely, I remained in it much longer than it was healthy to do so. I held onto things and people physically and emotionally. I later realised in order to learn and grow as a human being; we must let go of people and situations that no longer serve us. Simple as it may sound it can be an extremely difficult and challenging thing to actually do and follow through. One big lesson I did learn from this is that it's better to feel lonely on your own than to feel lonely when you are with someone.

*

The reason that I was selling my family home was that Graham and I had decided to move in together. I was excited and eager to start this new chapter with him, and as it worked out, a fresh start in a new home with him was the best thing I did. We loved each other unconditionally and although I know I did the hard work on myself, the counselling, the physical and psychological job of decluttering, I couldn't have done it without Graham's love. I was and still am so grateful for that. Our plans and dreams for the future allowed me to let go of my much-loved family home. I realised that our memories are not in bricks and mortar but can be carried anywhere in our hearts.

On the night I left the house where I grew up, I walked slowly down the stairs for the last time. I told myself I wasn't going to look back and I didn't, because that is what I had been doing the past fourteen years of my life and it was time to move forward. I loved living with Graham, his flat was across the road from the Viccy, so I hadn't ventured very far in my move. I was still doing the counselling, by this stage, the sessions were monthly, and I was on my second year of studying. I was back in Ward 15 only months after the discharge lounge secondment when an opportunity came up for a specialist stroke nurse which was a Monday to Friday post. I knew it was the right thing to do. It was now time to leave the wards and have a better work/life balance. It was still part of the Viccy, but the job was situated in a building across the road, called The Mansionhouse Unit. This was a Care of the Elderly unit which housed eight wards, one of which being the stroke Unit. I didn't know though if I had the energy to do an interview or face the idea of a new role. I still felt utterly exhausted at times and the dizzy spells were still occurring regularly.

The interview itself was a blur, I was off sick prior to it with dizziness and nausea, and I didn't think I had the strength to perform well at an interview. With the help from my good friend Christina though, we got a presentation together and I got the job. Looking back there is no doubt in my mind I should have taken a much longer period of sick time, between the anxiety, counselling and studying. I still felt an element of shame. What would people think? How could the ward survive without me? I don't necessarily think that was an ego thing, but more related to that sense of responsibility/ guilt and need to be helping others. I just kept going and pushing myself too hard. It was like being on a treadmill that I couldn't get off.

CHAPTER 15

Changing Lanes

Before I started the new job in late October 2005, Graham and I booked a three-week trip to Canada. I envisaged it to be an amazing trip, touring lots of different parts but unfortunately my anxiety was quite acute at that time. All I wanted to do was sleep. I would love to go back there someday and see it all again properly. I remember the beautiful Rocky Mountains and the resorts of Whistler and Lake Louise in particular. Hiring a car and listening to Bruce Springsteen whilst we drove through some breath-taking scenery but just wanting to sleep and feeling so guilty about how this was impacting Graham's holiday.

I started my new post a couple of days after returning from Canada. It was difficult at first, adapting to a slower pace, my body and mind were used to running around and dealing with stressful and challenging situations daily, but I enjoyed a lot of aspects of it and especially the Friday feeling that people talk about. I took regular breaks and finished most days on time, so it definitely led to a better work/life balance. Even with the ongoing issues, I really enjoyed working there. I knew I had made the right decision to leave the wards. With the absence of shift work and after selling my family home and moving in with Graham, I gradually started to feel better. I reduced the propranolol medication, and I made important changes to my lifestyle, continuing to stay off the cigarettes and majorly reducing my alcohol intake. I had come to realise that alcohol had been a trigger for me on so many occasions, which would only result in restlessness and agitation and so reducing this was so beneficial to my health. Since then, I enjoy a glass or two at most of wine or gin on an occasional basis now. I am much more aware that alcohol is still a trigger for me, as it can be for a lot of people. For me it's just not worth the feeling the next day. I used alcohol in the past, as a teenager, in my nurse training and in my twenties and early thirties to be sociable like many, to give me that boost of confidence and to numb the feelings of sadness and grief.

Alcohol is a depressant, and it can give you a very short feeling of relaxation but that quickly goes and for someone like me with had anxiety, you are left with a hangover that intensifies those anxious thoughts. There is a growing trend now for people who have decided to abstain from alcohol, perhaps as a temporary measure and then noticed quite dramatic health benefits, such as better sleep and increased energy. Cutting down my intake has certainly benefitted me.

After a few months or so, I settled into the new post, and I really felt a valued member there. I thoroughly enjoyed working with the nursing and medical staff and I worked closely alongside the multidisciplinary team, speech and language therapists, physiotherapists, occupational therapists and social workers. Everyone's input was fundamental to the rehabilitation and long-term care of the patients, and I developed a greater appreciation for the work that these therapists do. Although my anxiety persisted, I began to feel and notice glimmers of hope, happiness and a contentment that were previously unfamiliar to me.

During that time, a new addition was added to the family. My sister Yvonne had a baby, a wee precious bundle called Rachel. Another beautiful niece.

CHAPTER 16

Come What May

Graham surprised me that year, after our Canada trip, booking a night away on Christmas Eve at a beautiful hotel in the West end of Glasgow, I was bursting with excitement. We had spoken about our future together, but it still came as a surprise when he proposed to me that night after a romantic meal. He saw me at my best, running a ward, caring for others, the life and soul of the party but he was the one who also saw me at my most vulnerable, when I had no energy, was compassion fatigued and utterly distressed with anxiety and grief. I knew then that if he could love me and accept me with everything that had gone on, then we had a good solid foundation going forward. I had no doubt that I wanted to spend the rest of my life with him.

Our wedding was booked for ten months later. We didn't want to wait long. We were keen to start our own family and I was thirty-four when we got married. 2006 was a whirlwind of a year, a new job, the excitement of planning our wedding, and continuing studying. My sister Christine helped me so much, bridal dress shopping and her very honest opinions were valued and humorous. She needed no words; her face just said it all. I cherish all those memories and she did me the honour of walking me down the aisle too.

It was one of the best days of my life, surrounded by family and friends. It was also though tinged with sadness obviously with my mum and dad's absence. It was the main reason I did a speech on our wedding day to commemorate them. I had my mum and dad there beside me in spirit though, of that I am certain. We got married in Holy Cross Church in Dixon Avenue on the southside of Glasgow, the church where my own mum and dad had married and where I sang in the choir. It was the perfect day, despite the cold and rain. A piper welcomed everyone, and my friend Noreen read an Irish blessing as a tribute to my roots.

*

An Irish Blessing:

May the roads rise to meet you.
May the wind be always at your back.
May the sunshine warm upon your face.
The rain falls soft upon your fields and until we meet again.
May God hold you in the palm of his hands.

*

I felt loved, supported and cherished. My counselling came to an end in November 2006, a month after Graham and I got married. I was aware Jan had to end the counselling relationship. I was apprehensive and quite fearful because she had been that constant support, and I knew myself I could become dependent on her. I have never forgotten her and the impact she and the counselling process had on me. I talked openly about my grief and fears to her in a way in which I had never done before. She made me realise and understand that I was allowed to feel all the emotions I did without guilt or shame. She allowed me a safe space to grieve and move forward and I will forever be grateful to her for that.

CHAPTER 17
Body and Mind Connection

By the Springtime of 2006, although I had made significant lifestyle changes and felt emotionally better, I was still exhausted. It was starting to affect my mood. Although it wasn't like before when I had depression, I was beginning to get weary and frustrated with it all. I was trying so hard. Using my lightbox and having early nights. I began to wonder if my diet was a factor too. I spoke to my friend Colette about it who said she knew several people who had been to see someone for nutritionist advice. Her name was Claire Tomlins. I contacted her to arrange an appointment. She explained that she wasn't in fact a nutritionist but a kinesiologist but would be happy to see me if I wanted.

Kinesiology is a holistic therapy, there are different types, but all involve testing muscles to determine imbalances in the body which can be affecting the individuals mental and physical health. I started to go for sessions with Claire and it was probably at this point that I started to fully understand the significance of the body and mind connection.

Over the years, all the stressful and traumatic things I had seen as a nurse and personal loss had accumulated. Once I saw them all down on paper and I began talking about them, I began to understand how we store trauma and emotions in the body. This began my interest and journey into the complimentary and holistic approach to life. There was little wonder she said I was exhausted. She did indeed as part of the initial sessions discuss some intolerances to food and appropriate foods for me to increase my energy. In addition to the fact that the kinesiology sessions benefitted me, I have no doubt that Claire's caring and compassionate nature were fundamental in my slow recovery to better physical and emotional health. She planted many seeds of personal development for me, the importance of gratitude, what foods to eat or avoid, listening to my body and she also gave me like Jan, my counsellor had done, the space to listen without judgement. She gave me the green light to rest properly and look after myself, not just others.

During that time, I was off work again with a dental abscess. I was run down and overwhelmingly tired. It was relentless. I went to my GP after finishing my dental treatment as I didn't have the energy to do anything. I left the surgery that day with a prescription, (but not for medication), for exercise! He told me, no matter how I felt, I had to go out and walk for thirty minutes a day. He was kind but firm! It was a daunting task most days and hiding under the duvet covers and blankets was certainly more appealing. It didn't completely stop the fatigue issues, but it certainly helped. I pushed myself every day, and gradually with the kinesiology and my increase in exercise with walking and healthier lifestyle I slowly began to see an increase in energy levels. It was, however, a relocation to another city in the summer of that year, that began another whole new chapter of discovery and at last some respite from the burnout of life and work.

CHAPTER 18

Ferry Cross the Mersey

Graham was now nearing the end of his SHO post, and the next step was a four-year Registrar post in his chosen field of Palliative Care, to qualify as a consultant. He had applied for several positions in Leeds, Glasgow, Newcastle and Liverpool. I hoped he would be successful in one that required a move away so I could leave my job. If we had remained in Glasgow, although I was happy there, I knew I needed a career break. It was Liverpool that was lucky enough to get him and we left our home in August 2007. It was hard saying goodbye to family and friends, but I always knew it was just a chapter in my life and it wouldn't be forever.

My counsellor Jan's words came back to me when I found out we were leaving Glasgow, she had asked in one of our sessions, *"If you were to leave your job, what would it mean for you."*

"Freedom" I answered immediately. The move to Liverpool enabled me to feel that freedom from so many things, both personally and professionally.

Football, Brookside, the Beatles, Gerry Marsden's *Ferry Cross the Mersey* and *You'll Never Walk Alone*, were about the extent of what I knew about Liverpool prior to our move there. We visited it several times before relocating to look at rental accommodation. The city was preparing to be the European City of Culture the following year in 2008, just like Glasgow had done eighteen years previously. Areas of the city which appeared run down were rejuvenated and we saw each time we went, the transformation taking shape. There was an excitement in the air, we particularly loved it down at the docks. It was somewhere where we would often go over the years that we lived there. I loved showing off my adopted city, to friends and family who visited us. We did the Beatles tour and open-air bus tours. What made it though was the warmth of the people. I loved the scousers.

*

On the eighteenth anniversary of my dad's death, we went on our first trip on the actual ferry that takes you across the river from Wirral where we then lived, to Liverpool docks. We disembarked to Gerry and the pacemaker's iconic song Ferry Cross the Mersey. My last trip and the only one I can remember with just me and my dad, several years before he died, was aboard the Waverley. This is the oldest paddle steamer and does tours all round Scotland.

I wanted to do something on his anniversary that reminded me of him and that special day we had spent together when I was a teenager. He had been dead for the same length of time he had been in my life, and although I had a great sadness about that, I also knew that my dad would have been so pleased that I had met such a loving and caring man as Graham. Friends and family came to Liverpool regularly which was fun and appreciated and I also began to finally relax.

I only had one more module to complete my degree in nursing and so rather than transferring to John Moore University in Liverpool, I decided to finish it in Glasgow. I travelled up weekly for twelve weeks on the train, returning the same day. It was when I did this last module, Caring through Arts and Humanities, that I realised the power of words and I was struck by how much pleasure that I derived from writing. It felt powerful and cathartic. Studying for this module didn't just mean I would complete my degree; it transformed my way of looking at the world. The essays in the past had been a means to an end, to pass a module and move on to the next. This one was different though; part of the module was reading a book and writing a reflective piece.

I chose the Platform Ticket by the author, Dr Derek Doyle, a retired palliative care consultant. Graham had been given this book by a colleague after deciding to specialise in this field. Dr Doyle shares his personal insights and memories whilst working in St Columba's Hospice in Edinburgh.

The title The Platform Ticket draws on an analogy by a patient, that in the past, people would buy a platform ticket to accompany someone before they boarded their train journey. The patient draws a comparison between this and her own final days of life. There are many recurring themes throughout the book, including spirituality, quality of life, as well as moral and ethical dilemmas. What is evident in every chapter is the overwhelming feeling of caring and being there for patients and their loved ones during end-of-life care. Having had my own deeply personal experience of palliative care with my mum as well as professional experience, the book totally resonated with me. Dr Doyle acknowledges his skills and expertise but realises that it is the patients themselves who taught him. A view shared by me wholeheartedly. The book provides a genuine and compassionate depiction of the atmosphere within a hospice and the principles that palliative care strives to uphold. Although the book is about death, it unequivocally celebrates the essence of life.

During my trips between Liverpool and Glasgow I had more time, no work commitments and so for the first time in the four years of my nursing degree, I was able to take time to write and reflect. I had the privilege of purchasing so many platform tickets in my career. It was undoubtedly the most rewarding piece of work I ever did, and I knew at that stage that I wanted to turn my dream of writing into one day into a reality. I also wrote about stress and anxiety for the other part of the module. I was becoming increasingly aware of how they were both becoming more and more common in society. I still felt a degree of stigma attached to my own anxiety and depression. I stumbled across a quote by Alfred D Souza, an inspirational writer and philosopher which really resonated with me.

*

"Happiness is a journey, not a destination."

*

This, at the age of 36 was an epiphany for me. It put everything into context and made complete sense. Most people say, when I meet the one or when I change jobs or move house then I will be happy. I'm sure most of the population if asked what's the one thing you would like to be, they would say happy. This introduced me to inspirational quotes and positive affirmations which I still use to this day. This remains one of my most favourite quotes.

I felt justifiably proud of my achievement of completing my degree. It was monumental for me. It wasn't really the degree itself or the graduation ceremony that I was proud of. It was the actual accomplishing it despite the obstacles and challenges I had faced throughout it. I started to write after I did this essay about losing my parents, nursing, my burnout, anxiety, and the dream of one day writing a book. I knew I had a lot of life experiences, a lot of grief and sadness but equally I had experienced just as much joy, happiness and contentment.

CHAPTER 19

Grief

Perhaps the most well-known theory on grief that was around during my period of counselling was from Elizabeth Kubler Ross, a Swiss born psychiatrist who proposed the five common stages of grief. These were actually intended for patients who had received a cancer diagnosis (I only learnt this recently) and were not necessarily for families of people who had died but it did help me. Denial, anger, bargaining, depression and acceptance are the five she suggested. These of course are non-linear, people can experience these aspects at different times, and they don't come in a specific order. She suggested that you can go back and forwards and even miss a stage. At some level it helped me, as it made me feel that what I was going through was normal. It was a huge step for me in understanding grief and the emotions we go through.

Grief of course is not just associated with dying. It's a response to the loss of someone or something that was important- divorce, homelessness, a diagnosis of life-threatening illness, miscarriage. Grief affects people in different ways to varying degrees and it can often descend on you like a dark cloud. We must learn to adapt, to live our lives without that person or indeed in the case of miscarriage what could have been. The ending of a partnership or a change in body image or an adaption to a different way of life after an illness are all examples of grief that can feel as if our hearts are breaking. It's not about forgetting or suddenly getting over your grief but more like moving/ weaving your way through it. Slowly, like a toddler learning to walk, taking baby steps and not beating yourself up when you sometimes stumble and fall. What no one really talks about though is how exhausting grief can be.

There can also be a sense of guilt associated with moving on with our lives. I remember often, particularly in the early years after my mum and dad died of sometimes feeling that I shouldn't be having this much fun or enjoyment of life. It was as if at some level, I felt disrespectful that I hadn't mourned them enough. I would imagine though that anyone whom we have loved and lost would want us to enjoy our lives and move forward. It doesn't mean they are forgotten; just that we must learn to live without them, which is probably the hardest road we travel in life.

Delayed grief or complicated grief is the late or prolonged reaction to the loss of a loved one or thing. It's normal for grief to cause pain, extreme emotion and difficulty but delayed grief can manifest unexpectedly and potentially harm a person's mental well-being and health. This is what I believe I experienced after losing my mum and dad.

Anticipatory, or living grief is where someone experiences feelings of loss before a person dies, possibly a long before the time of death. This could be a family member of possibly someone with dementia, a terminal illness or a lifelong disability. People can feel guilt for this. Indeed, from an external perspective, their loved one remains physically present.

Others might not even recognise that they are undergoing a grief reaction.

On reflection, during the time of my mum's terminal diagnosis, I didn't think I had an outlet for my grief, I didn't want to burden my mum and dad. How could I when the grief was all about them. I cried and raged at the weekends readily with alcohol, my way of coping I guess with the enormity of this anticipatory grief. People often would say to me that they don't know how I coped, but I am aware that I always had people that loved me, and I am grateful for the love and friendship that surrounded me. I am sure this helped me to keep going.

CHAPTER 20

Helping and Elfing

Graham and I bought our first home together in Irby, in Wirral, six months later in January 2008. We were keen to settle down and have our own family. I underwent fertility investigations and hormone medication as I was having difficulty in conceiving. During that period, emotions ran high, largely due to the medications I was taking. My hormones were fluctuating wildly, leading to days of stability, followed by sudden bouts of sadness and emptiness. After several months, I needed to get out there, make friends, work and have some fun in amongst all the medical stuff involved in helping me to conceive.

I decided to become a volunteer; it gave me something to do and a sense of purpose. Helplink was a local organisation in Irby which provided transport, shopping and befriending services and I spent about eighteen months there. I did one full day a week. I did food shopping for some elderly people but mainly it was befriending visits in nursing homes or to people in their own homes. I used to go regularly to see a lady called Mary who lived in a nursing home as her family all lived far away. I would go and see her in her room or on a nice day, take her out in the garden in her wheelchair. She loved seeing all the flowers and getting fresh air. Graham was working Christmas Day that year, so I spent a couple of hours with her in the afternoon as she wasn't seeing any family. It was incredibly special, and she made my day as much as I made hers. The staff were very caring, and I was always welcomed. We both got a lot out of those visits. I thoroughly enjoyed my time spent with Mary and the other people.

This was my second experience of volunteering, the first was in 1993 after I qualified. There was a period of around six weeks or so before I started in the nursing home in Darnley, and I decided I wanted to give something back to the hospice where my mum had died. Looking back on this experience, I realised that it was perhaps too soon after my mum's death to become so closely involved in that kind of work. Doing voluntary work can be so rewarding, whatever you do and something I recommend so much. It is about giving something back and whatever you give, whether it's a couple of hours working in a charity shop, caring or helping with homeless people it is worthwhile. No act of kindness is ever wasted.

When I was in my late twenties, I experienced an incredibly lonely period, despite having so many people around me. The difference being though is that I had the choice of meeting friends for coffee or a walk or to go to the pub. A lot of people don't have that luxury due to a variety of factors. They may be isolated due to physical restrictions like poor mobility, dementia or psychological issues, confidence or poor mental health, poverty etc.

*

I was keen to use this time of not working to learn new skills and having an interest in life coaching, I began a twelve-week introductory course in Cheshire. I started to look at situations and relationships differently after this. I completed many varying courses over the years which had enhanced my skills and knowledge including an accredited counselling skills course in 1998 and my nursing degree, but it was undoubtedly this life coaching course in 2008 that helped transform my way of thinking. Whilst I believe that a positive approach to life is important, I also recognise that this is not necessarily easy to do, especially if you have low moods, anxiety or life appears difficult. I was often prone to imagining the worst-case scenario, however, I found that changing my perspective and learning to expect the best outcome is a healthier way for my mind.

At this time, I was also becoming more and more interested in the mind and body connection and in the benefits of complementary therapies. I started to attend holistic events. I had a day out in Manchester at a wellbeing fayre and it was there that I experienced Reiki for the first time. My interest in complementary therapies had grown after I could see how the Kinesiology had benefitted me. I was blown away in that twenty-minutes Reiki taster session. It was busy and noisy at the fayre, there were loud gongs, speakers and the sound of lots of people, but lying down on that couch the noise completely faded into the background. I felt peaceful and I experienced tremendous heat particularly around my stomach and groin area. I had suffered from intense mid cycle pain since puberty known as mittelschmerz, the German name for middle pain and the medical investigations which I was having for infertility showed I had a degree of endometriosis.

Reiki means Universal Life Energy and is a Japanese technique for stress reduction and relaxation that promotes healing. It is holistic and works on the mind, body and spirit by stimulating a person's own natural healing abilities. I had a gut feeling that there was something to this Reiki. I had additional sessions after that initial introduction and attended sporadically thereafter. Every session was different, but I always felt relaxed and focused after it. I had no idea at that stage of what an important part Reiki would play in my life.

I enrolled in the nurse bank at the local hospital in Wirral after six months or so of settling into our new home. I planned to do a couple shifts there a week. After completing an introductory week, I waited to hear back. I became increasingly bored waiting for the lengthy paperwork to be completed and I needed something to do other than the voluntary work. I came across an advertisement for a seasonal job with Santa one day when browsing through a local paper. Before you could say "HO HO HO" I was on the phone and had got an interview. I got an Elf position and worked for a six-week period in the John Lewis department store in Liverpool. The grotto was quite something! it was magical, with twinkly lights, a winter wonderland and you were immediately catapulted back to that feeling of anticipation and excitement as a small child. My job was to assist the big man, giving out presents to the kids, being cheery and pulling funny faces to make the kids smile for pictures. It was a great laugh with all the staff and my Glaswegian accent went down a treat. I was asked on several occasions to say two phrases. "There's been a murder" being the first one which is a nod to the brilliant Scottish actor Mark McManus who played the lead role in the long running detective series Taggart. The second was Curly Wurley. Curly Wurley sounds so different in a scouse accent than a Glaswegian one! The grotto could get quite manic at times and some parents were completely over the top, forcing their screaming kids to sit on Santa's knees- whether they liked it or not. Sometimes I felt a bit tense when I was on the meet and greet at the entrance on the till. I could see the queue round the corner and the impatience from the kids and the adults was intense. I had to remind myself though that I had been a team leader, assisted in cardiac arrests and medical emergencies, chased big strapping men with alcohol withdrawal down fire escapes, so I could definitely cope with this! Being one of Santa's helpers was fun and joyous most of the time and it was great not being in a serious role for the first time in my adulthood. I really embraced it. So much so, that Mike the photographer called me to come back the following year. However, by that time I was eight months pregnant and so this wasn't possible. Happy days indeed! I did this elf job impulsively and I was so glad I did. I received a call around mid-December to say that I could now start my bank nursing post in Arrowe Park hospital. They wanted me to start immediately, but I declined as I had committed to being an elf and knew I could not neglect this important duty. I am not sure the hospital had ever heard of that as an excuse before! Well, I couldn't let Santa down, could I? Every year since then, I proudly put the picture of Santa and I, pride of place on the mantlepiece at Christmas.

*

Doing this job was a welcome distraction from an incredibly busy year, moving house and having investigations and medications, all of which were unpleasant and emotional but necessary to help us with our dream of having a baby. I started the nursing bank shifts in January 2009 but only worked there for a few months as I became pregnant in March of that year. This was at the time of the swine flu outbreak, so I didn't go back. I didn't want to take the risk. I had a happy and healthy pregnancy despite my journey to motherhood being a difficult one. Katie was our miracle baby. That year I began to feel much healthier, physically and mentally. Being pregnant also brought great friendships through ante natal classes. All in all, it was an exciting and special time in my life.

CHAPTER 21

The Greatest Day

Our daughter Katie was born in November 2009, weighing in at 5lbs 13 oz. That was a shock, as I was told repeatedly that I was carrying a big baby. I found it overwhelming after she was born. In a four bedded room, exhausted and sore after birth, she was so tiny, and I was terrified of holding her. The midwives were extremely supportive and caring. The acute anxiety that I had experienced before in Glasgow returned with a vengeance.

I couldn't cope with the noise of the other babies crying and the hyper alert way I felt. I was moved to a side room, when it became available that night, but in spite of this, I didn't sleep at all. Katie was looked after by the midwives. The anxiety continued and I was kept in with Katie for three nights whilst they monitored her blood sugars and helped me with breast feeding. Faced now with this terror and anxiety again, coupled with the hormonal dip after giving birth, I was experiencing extreme distress and now, I was responsible for this new baby. The dizziness, nausea and pacing began again. I was overwhelmed by the responsibility; no classes can prepare you for that. I knew though getting back to Graham and my own surroundings would definitely help me to cope. They were a terrifying few days and I was desperate to get back home. Even though this anxious experience was really scary and not what any new mum would want, I knew deep down that it would pass, and it wouldn't be like the prolonged anxiety I had experienced in the past. The day that Graham and I got home, we placed Katie in the living room in her car seat, looked at each other and nervously laughed. *"What do we do now."* Even through that fog of sleep deprivation and hormonal changes, I did quickly settle, and my anxiety levels gradually left me.

My confidence grew over the weeks and months as a mum and I believe that as I was older, (even though I was a first-time mum) and going through the process of everything we did, I didn't feel under any sort of pressure. I was doing it my way, winging it mostly, doing most of the things that you're not apparently supposed to do, depending on what book you read or whose opinion you listen too. So, I have to admit that Katie was in our bed for naptimes and most bedtimes.

Graham worked long hours and it could be lonely at times, but I chose to see the positives in it. I didn't feel any pressure as some mums may do. When you're sleep deprived, your child has colic and your breast feeding 24/7, (or so it feels), you must do what's right for your own wee family. I think as I was thirty-seven when I had Katie and it had taken me so long to conceive, (although in effect it was two years which is nothing compared to some) as a result, I didn't sweat the small stuff. We, as everyone does though, got through it, the sleepless nights and endless feeds. Once I got home from hospital I began to settle almost immediately in my own surroundings and my fear turned into the most profound love I could ever have imagined.

That year was a particularly bad winter and so cold with lots of snow. I cooried in with Katie. Eat, sleep, repeat. Maybe if I had been at home in Glasgow when Katie was born, I would have found the visits overwhelming. However, by the time February came for her christening, I kind of felt I knew what I was doing as a mum. Most of the time it was just me and Katie. I treasured that. It was the most exhausting but most rewarding thing I've ever done.

When Katie was two years old, I was feeling she needed to mix more with other kids and for me to have some time apart from her. She joined a wonderful playgroup called Auntie Liz's, which was a total Godsend. As she had been with me though 24/7 for over two years, needless to say, she was not enamoured when I left her. During her first settling in morning, I got a call to say to come back earlier. I could hear her crying as I got out the car. We tried over the coming weeks to leave her for short periods, but she was having none of it! So, the result was, another stint of volunteering. This time at Katies playgroup for two years, one morning a week. We gradually increased Katie's time there to twice a week, and I helped once weekly. Another new experience for me and a newfound respect for folk who work with preschool children.

CHAPTER 22

An Invisible Loss

As our journey to parenthood hadn't been easy, Graham and I knew there may be difficulty in conceiving again. We decided to try for another baby after Katie was two years old. We were over the moon when I became pregnant naturally in the spring of 2012. We were so looking forward to a sibling for Katie and another baby to complete our family. I felt well through the first trimester and had quite a noticeable bump, so we were totally devastated and shocked at the twelve-week scan when there was no heartbeat detected. I remember the sonographer just saying, *"I'm so sorry."* I had genuinely never even contemplated the idea of miscarriage, even though I was nearly forty by this stage. I naively thought because of everything we had been through first time round to have Katie, and having such a healthy pregnancy that I would be ok. Time literally stood still. We were ushered into a private room, Katie was with us, and it was totally surreal. Our happy toddler, laughing and playing at our feet, whilst the midwife spoke. I couldn't take it in what she was saying. We went home that Friday afternoon just utterly numb. The sun was shining on that July day, but all

I could feel was darkness and despair. I somehow had to make the decision whether to go ahead with surgery or allow nature as it were to take its course. I opted for the surgery and was booked in as a day case patient for the following week. There had been no warning signs, no bleeding or anything untoward to suggest there was anything wrong with our baby. This is known as a silent miscarriage.

I had to sit in the same waiting room in the pre op clinic where less than a week before we had sat as excited expectant parents. There was a certain cruelty to that. I tried desperately hard not to look at the pregnant mums who surrounded me. The next few weeks and months were so hard. I celebrated my fortieth birthday weeks later, and friends came down from Glasgow. I appreciated them coming so much and we all had a lovely night, but everything was just tinged with sadness. I still had hope though, hope that there was still time and that I could become pregnant again. The Fertility clinic advised however to proceed to IVF, which we did at the end of the same year. I have nothing but the highest praise and gratitude for the compassionate and professional care both Graham and I received from Arrowe Park hospital in Wirral and The Women's Hospital in Liverpool but perhaps on reflection, it had been too soon emotionally and physically.

Throughout the IVF process I just got on with it, my main concern was always Katie. I had some friends in Wirral who helped me enormously by looking after Katie when I was at all the different appointments. This is when my home sickness really came into play for me though. There was a constant cycle of appointments, with frequent trips for scans and blood tests and the inevitable, interminable waiting for results. The hardest part of the whole IVF process was the two weeks wait after the embryo transfer, to see if all the trips, hormones, and prayers have worked. It seemed like an eternity, riding an emotional rollercoaster with your hormones fluctuating and just everything you put into it physically and emotionally for both Graham and me.

We were overjoyed to discover at the beginning of December that the IVF had been successful, but sadly our joy was short lived. On New Year's Day 2013, I started bleeding. We went to the hospital and were totally devastated when they broke the news that I had miscarried. I asked if they could scan me again, just to make sure. I went to the toilet, grabbing onto the walls to steady myself on the way. It felt like an out of body experience. Another internal scan confirmed what deep down I already knew. I had further surgery, but this time was different from previously. I became extremely unwell within twenty- four hours and had to be admitted to hospital with a high temperature and severe abdominal pain. I was put on intravenous fluids and antibiotics, given morphine and the pain eventually settled. But there was real concern that I may have to have more surgery. Thankfully though this didn't happen. I had developed an infection post operatively during the dilation and curettage (D and C) This is a procedure carried out for some women after miscarriage which carries a small risk of infection after it. I was in hospital for several days in a gynaecology ward, in a single room. I was monitored regularly for blood pressure and temperature observations, but no one ever asked how I was emotionally. I felt extremely vulnerable as a patient and to be honest quite let down. I was used to being the one giving care not the one receiving it. The medical care had been great and professional, but I felt there was no real empathy or compassion from the ward nurses that looked after me. When you have suffered a loss like this, you just want to be in your own bed and own home to process your grief. It was a long and anguished few days. I remember walking to the toilet the day after admission and seeing a young girl in the main ward. She was on oxygen and had all sorts of infusions with several family members surrounding her bed, all so worried looking. I think for the first time in my life I felt profoundly grateful to be alive. Yes, I was devastated and sore, but I knew I would be ok in time, and I was so thankful for the gift of having Katie. Graham looked exhausted, he was naturally worrying about me and worrying about work too. He had recently just become a consultant in Palliative Care and was also the Clinical Lead of Woodlands Hospice in Aintree, all whilst studying for a master's degree!

I think men can often be neglected with miscarriage. They have lost too; the emphasis is usually always on the mum and her feelings and grief. I don't think I appreciated this particularly well at the time. We were both devastated and coped in our own ways. Graham had some health issues of his own after that and I'm sure this was a reaction to what we were going through, his loss and the worry about me.

Katie wasn't used to being apart from me, but Graham and his mum did a wonderful job of looking after us both when I was in hospital and in the days that followed. I just wanted to be home, lie in my own bed and not face the world. There was no choice in the matter though, I had to keep going, for our daughter and for Graham.

*

Years later, I realised that what I went through was similar to that year of 1990 and 1991 when I did not have time to mourn one huge personal loss as another came right after. I felt a pressure due to my age to move forward quickly and so within six months I experienced two miscarriages, underwent IVF and had two surgeries. We attended the miscarriage clinic later that year, even though this was only my second miscarriage but due to my age and previous fertility issues we were referred there and seen quickly. Normally women don't tend to be seen until they have suffered three miscarriages as sadly miscarriage is more common than people realise but it's so hard for people who go through this process to have to wait. It is estimated that one in eight pregnancies will result in miscarriage and perhaps higher numbers as some women do not realise, they are pregnant. All my bloods were fine when I was assessed, which I was told was a good thing, and there seemed to be no real explanation as to why it had happened. Somehow, I just accepted this. It was no one's fault. I still had hope. We decided though not to proceed with anymore IVF and we tried to be positive that I would conceive naturally again. We were offered counselling but didn't take the offer up. On reflection, this may have been something which would have helped but I just wanted to get on with it. Time was not on our side, and deep down I felt I couldn't face more counselling. The thought of those floodgates opening again was too overwhelming for me. I just had to keep going and stay focused. Pregnancy loss is so so hard to describe, it is an invisible loss. The few days immediately after you miscarry are a whirlwind of emotions, the disbelief, the anguish. There is also the sharp drop in pregnancy hormones which can mean a major dip in your mood. The combination of the drop in hormones and trying to process the loss is exhausting and I felt so vulnerable. Some people never speak of their loss and some people are never really the same, so please be mindful of other's feelings. A childless couple may not be through choice, and neither are parents with one child always either! I never really spoke about how I felt with many people until now. Maybe if you are thinking of asking someone when they are having kids or when is the next one coming, the advice is simple, DONT! and never assume anything. Everyone's grief is different.

It can be a dark and lonely place when trying to conceive and/or have pregnancy loss. I struggled at times with other pregnancies and babies being born. It's not their child you want; I was genuinely pleased for them, but it serves as a reminder of what could have been. Not having my own mum to chat with throughout the process made me miss her even more. I always appreciated the daughter I had and the loving relationship with Graham but comments like *"at least you have Katie"* weren't helpful. I was aware of this, but by others (and myself saying this) it suppressed grief yet again. Yes, I did have a child, but I was entitled to grieve what I had lost.

I recently came across a booklet called Miscarriage and early baby loss by Breda Theakston. It explains what a miscarriage is and the impact it can have on the parents and family members, it offers gentle and compassionate information and advice. It is certainly something I think I would have benefitted from reading after ours.

Throughout this process though and despite all that we were experiencing, we were a happy wee trio, Graham, Katie and me. However, I knew after this we really needed to come back home to Scotland…

CHAPTER 23
Caledonia

While we lived in Wirral, we travelled back and forth to Scotland at least three or four times a year, for family events and holidays. It's partly what kept me going. We had a playlist in the car. Lots of Scottish songs. *Caledonia* by Dougie McLean, Runrig's *Loch Lomond* and *Dignity* by Deacon Blue to name a few. My heart soared every time we passed the border, seeing the beautiful blue and white saltire flag.

We had never really celebrated the famous Scottish poet, Rabbie Burns when we lived in Scotland, although we had got married in his hometown of Alloway at the picturesque Brig A Doon. The year after Katie was born though, we decided to have a Burns supper at our house, inviting three couples we had met from ante natal classes. Graham had his kilt on, addressing the haggis like a pro and we ceilidh danced and had brilliant fun. We got our Scouse friends to read aloud Burns poetry in their best Scottish accent, which hysterically ranged from sounding like Welsh to Indian. I'm always proud to be Scottish but that night, it felt like we did our glorious nation proud.

Sometimes the homesickness would just come from nowhere, a longing that seemed to pervade everything. We went to a deer centre in the Scottish Perthshire hills when Katie was around three on one of our regular visits home. It was a glorious sunny day, and I just suddenly became aware of all this lush green and the rolling hills surrounding us. I ached, physically and emotionally, to return to the motherland.

Graham first applied for a post back in Glasgow, in 2013, He wasn't successful and at first, we were bitterly disappointed. We knew after this that a job in Scotland was the right thing for us and my mums saying *"what's for you, won't go by you"* was often quoted. We just had to bide our time.

But we knew it had to be the right job and right for us as a family.

One morning, as I sat in the car with Katie, on my daily journey to get her to sleep, I asked out loud for a sign.

"Will we get back to Scotland?" A formation of clouds gathered as a cross, against the backdrop of a beautiful clear blue sky. I looked up and there it was, my sign. The Saltire flag, Scotland's national flag. I knew at that point that we would someday soon go home. We are given signs all the time, if we stop and believe. Common ones are finding feathers or coins, which is a sign that we are being looked after. Every year since we moved to our first house, I have seen a white feather underneath my washing lines. Not anywhere else in the gardens of where we have lived but always where they will be noticed. It's a source of comfort and a reminder that love never dies.

Home will always be where Graham and Katie are, but we really wanted to come back to Scotland before she started primary school. I am so grateful for our time in Liverpool and Wirral. I have no doubt that our move there was the key in us having Katie, and for that I will always be eternally thankful.

*

In 2014 there was the exciting possibility for Graham of two consultant posts in Ayrshire or Glasgow. I somehow managed to persuade him to put our house on the market before he was even given any interviews! My thoughts were that I didn't want to wait until he had the job, and I was left in Wirral with Katie alone, trying to sell our home. We decided that even if we sold our home and he wasn't successful at interview then we would just rent. A lot of pressure for him on reflection. However, I had that sense of knowing, the vibes that it was the right thing to do and of course a lot of faith in Graham. He was successful in his interview for the Marie Curie Hospice in Glasgow, where he still works today. We were finally coming home!

*

Although we were delighted to be moving back after seven years, it was still a very stressful time. We had issues selling our property and we had to move into hospital accommodation for two months after the sale went through. Nonetheless, I saw the positives in the situation. Every day was a step closer to Glasgow. We moved back in October 2014.

The regular contact with friends in Glasgow was vitally important to me throughout that chapter in my life, perhaps more than any other time. There wasn't a week that went by that I didn't speak to at least two or three friends from home. In fact, a couple of friendships deepened as a result of the distance between us. My close friends knew the real Catriona, not the one who had to put on the mask. I made several good friends in Wirral, and I am grateful for all their love and support. The value of friendships is pivotal in our lives, from the ones we make in childhood, during our early years all the way through to adulthood. I have been blessed with many friendships in my life so far and although my circle has indeed grown smaller over the years, I understand now that people come into our lives for a reason, maybe even just for a season. I haven't necessarily ever fallen out with friends but like everything in life sometimes we fall away naturally. People can move away physically, but also emotionally. We all change as we get older, our priorities, how we view the world. It would be a boring world if we were all the same.

There are too many people to acknowledge here, with the risk of offending perhaps someone I haven't mentioned, but I have never forgotten kindness from friends. This is why, for me, friends became like family, especially after losing my parents. Despite the close relationship and shared grief with my sisters, I found it easier to speak honestly with friends about my own anguish.

Colette was my buddy, through secondary school. She is one of only a couple of friends I have that knew my mum and dad. She was a huge support to me when my parents died. She was my partner in crime, we were in the same class at Holyrood Secondary School. We weren't badly behaved pupils; we just liked to talk and have a laugh. I wouldn't say we were disruptive although our Maths teacher and Home Economics teacher may have thought differently! We grew closer in fifth and sixth year as the school started a project with older people which involved befriending. Every Friday we would go to the local bakers and get cakes and bring them to Mrs Friel who lived in Govanhill, near to the school. She was a special lady and not just anyone, but in fact she was Colette's Nana. She had the warmest smile and a twinkle in her eye. We would sit and chat with her for hours and watch TV together, mainly North and South with Patrick Swayze. I have very fond memories of those times. Working with older people and befriending featured later in my life and I believe a lot of that stemmed from those Friday afternoons.

During my training and nursing career, I met my nurse pals, and they helped me through the difficult times, as well as the party times We have different friends for different things. Ones we can have a good laugh with, ones with good advice or a shoulder to cry on. If you've got a friend or in my case a good few of these then you are blessed.

CHAPTER 24

Home

We moved into rented accommodation on our return to Glasgow and Katie started school a few days later. She took a while to adapt which was understandable as there had been many changes to her wee life. Night times were often a battlefield and shouts of *"I'm going back to Irby"* were commonplace. We spent the first few months settling in, a new job for Graham, a new area to live in. The sheer gratitude of popping over to see friends and family rather than the usual four-hour drive.

Shortly after returning, I became pregnant again for the fourth and sadly the last time. Again, I miscarried at six weeks. This last, final miscarriage was one of the toughest experiences I have faced in my life. For the first time ever, I began to feel worthless, Katie was at school all day and I didn't feel I really had a role. I wasn't a nurse now and didn't feel I wanted to return to the profession, and I couldn't seem to have another child. I had the excitement of having another baby and then when that was taken away, I felt bereft. I was forty-two years old by this stage.

Fortunately, I was spared the trauma of going through surgery again. I can only remember going to my friends' house and discovering I was bleeding. I drove home in a daze and called the early pregnancy unit who arranged for me to go in the following day for a scan. I can't recall any more details after that, the trip to the hospital, the scan, how they broke the news. I can remember in vivid detail the previous times but not this one. I am aware I have blocked it out as it was so emotionally traumatic for me. I knew that time was running out and I wondered how much more I could put my body and mind through. I felt it took me several months after each miscarriage, just to feel physically better. Emotionally, well that took a much longer time to heal.

I was home though in Glasgow and so thankful for that, and I had a beautiful daughter. I knew that I had to do something to make me feel better, that inner determination was still there, and I began to think about Reiki again. This time I wanted to learn it for myself, for self-healing, I just had to find the right teacher.

I went to a holistic fayre in the Trades Hall in Glasgow in June 2015, a few months after the miscarriage. There was a large display of the names of all the therapists and traders there that day. I was drawn to the name Lorna McLean. I spent hours there, wandering round, listening to the speakers, choosing beautiful shiny crystals, not necessarily knowing what healing properties they had but just knowing I was drawn to them. I started chatting to someone at one of the stalls and I told him I was interested in learning Reiki, and he said, *"You may want to speak to Lorna"* pointing to the lady next to him and I just knew. I had that sense of knowing again. You can meet someone and just click; someone that makes you feel good when you are around them. Well, that's Lorna. We had a chat, and I just felt a connection. She said she was teaching a Reiki class the following month, but I was under no pressure to sign up. She gave me her contact details and suggested I go away and think about it. I wandered around again but within a short period I went back. I didn't need time to think about it, I knew this was right to go with Lorna and so my Reiki journey began.

Healing dates back thousands of years. The Japanese word Reiki translates as Universal life force. It was discovered and developed early in the early 20th century by Mikao Usui. Whilst meditating on Mount Kurama in Japan in 1922 he experienced enlightenment and received the reiki energy. He developed his style of Reiki, Usui Reiki Ryoho. Although Reiki is a spiritual method of healing it is not affiliated or dependent upon any religious organisation. It's a non-invasive complementary therapy and can benefit everyone. It is known for its stress reducing benefits, stimulating the body's natural ability to heal itself.

*

Reiki 1 is the first foundation level of reiki when you receive the attunement/placement of Reiki into your own energy field which you then can connect with. The philosophy of Reiki is rooted in the five Principles that Mikao Usui devised and are taught and explained in First degree Reiki. They provide guidance for healing and balance and are translated as:

*

"The Secret art of inviting happiness, the miraculous medicine of all diseases":

*

Just for today, I will not worry,
Just for today, I will not anger,
Just for today, I will work honestly,

Just for today, I will be kind to others and all living things,
Just for today, I will be grateful for all I have."

*

I say these principles daily aloud, they encourage me to focus on the present moment, they are principles, not rules, but an essential and valued ingredient of my daily life and practice. Reiki never fails to amaze me and if used regularly, it can help us physically, spiritually and emotionally. It has been a constant in my life since connecting with it and I am grateful every day for it. I still have times like everyone where I can get uptight or stressed but knowing I have this wonderful gift of Reiki, instils a calmness inside me. It has been truly life changing. Reiki isn't just about a set of hand positions, seeing colours and feeling heat. It's about incorporating the principles as a way of life, being true to ourselves, of deep compassion and love for ourselves and others.

Reiki 1 was the start of my self-healing, it gave me back a sense of purpose and although I had to heal myself first, I knew this was something I wanted to share. I was able to do Reiki on myself and friends and family. I floated out of that special day at Lornas home, knowing that this was the start of something new and exciting. Despite my grief I felt I would be OK; it gave me hope.

CHAPTER 25

Hope

HOPE — what is it and what's its purpose? I've asked myself this often through the years. It's translation in the Oxford dictionary is *"a feeling of expectation and desire for a particular thing to happen."* It's such a small word, yet with such huge meaning.

Hope got me through those days after losing my mum and dad. I held onto the belief that I would meet someone loving and kind after the ending of a long-term relationship. Hope was there when I became exhausted with my job and lifestyle. Feeling I was on a treadmill, and I couldn't get off. Hope was also there throughout our journey to parenthood, being apart from family and friends and seeing those beautiful Scottish hills. Hope though, was what got me through our miscarriages. After each one I was devastated but I had always felt there would be another child for us. That didn't happen, so why did I hold on to something that ultimately didn't materialise?

Hope is to me what keeps us going when we have lost our way, when we feel burdened and in despair. It can help us get up in the morning, knowing brighter days are ahead and that after the dark there is always light. I couldn't imagine a life without it. It's as vital as love, gratitude and the air we breathe. I remind myself of this often now, that feelings of hopelessness or fear or what we regard as negative emotions, are exactly that, just feelings. Emotions, like everything are temporary.

Sometimes it's just not quite enough to hope though. We need to take positive steps ourselves to move forward, do something different. *"If you always do what you've always done, then you'll always get what you've always got"* is a great expression of initiating change for us. Reiki helped make this change for me.

There are many books written on manifesting and asking the universe to grant us what we desire but there also must be a level of responsibility from us. I am all for vision boards and journaling and asking for help with my dreams. Some requests have been granted, some I had to wait a long, long time for. However, that has taught me patience and again added a layer of gratitude. Some things haven't happened, but then other opportunities have arisen and maybe what we think we want is not always for our higher good. We usually get what we need not what we want. I've learnt through this journey that it's important, both to dream and to hope, but also that if it doesn't work out then it was not meant to be. There are lessons in everything.

CHAPTER 26

Gratitude

Expressing gratitude for me was the big game changer in my life. It's not that I didn't appreciate my life before I started Reiki, but when I began to acknowledge and express gratitude daily, it undoubtedly enhanced it.

I found many ways to do this. Writing every day in a journal and stating three things I am grateful for, as well as my thoughts, feelings and experiences of that day. At the end of every month, I reflect on all there is to be thankful for and then again at the end of the year. Naturally, my family and friends feature mostly in this journal, as do a lot of seasonal joys- the sun on my face, the beauty in nature and regular moments where I am grateful for the joy and gift of just being alive on this planet. I write often about being thankful for the gift of Reiki for self-care and to share with others.

Gratitude has given me a greater appreciation of all my senses and in particular my sense of hearing, listening to the birdsong, being in stillness, the silence and trusting my own inner voice, guiding me daily. Journalling each day can also be beneficial, in goal setting or in gaining insight into difficult situations or events. I think if I overcomplicate things or if a task takes too long then there is a tendency for me not to bother. So, setting aside five or ten minutes each day to write can make a difference. Small habits can be more productive and easier to achieve. It's building the habit that is key.

Another idea is to place a jar somewhere visible, perhaps on a mantlepiece or in the kitchen on the windowsill and filling it with pieces of paper with what you are grateful for. It can be seen every day, and it reminds you, despite the storms you may be facing, that there is always something to be grateful for.

I was brought up to be thankful by my parents. How we teach our children to acknowledge and express their gratitude is important along with kindness and empathy. A phrase my mum used to use often however was *"we all have our crosses to bear"* and many people to this day use this analogy. There is a religious connotation to this and a sense of being burdened. I cannot even begin to imagine what is like to live in poverty, be homeless, or in an abusive relationship or an individual fleeing a war-torn country, but for many this is a reality. We have witnessed refugees fleeing the country they have called home and being forced to leave their families and their life behind. Their journey is unimaginable.

Looking back, a big factor in why I didn't share with people how depressed or anxious I was or why I didn't take time off work was for that reason. I felt guilty about my grief as I was aware so many others were experiencing intense physical and emotional pain in my job as a nurse, in society and in the world around me. Their crosses seemed heavier, so how could I complain about mine? Yes, I had lost but so had many others, but I had a nice home with good family and friends, a job I loved and a great social life. How could I feel this way? Especially as so much time had passed since the events I was mourning for. I understand now that there is no time limit on grief. I am so grateful that I was able to move through it and finally acknowledge and accept my losses. I am also allowed to still feel sad and emotional too, whilst appreciating all I have. Again, life showing me that it's possible to experience vastly different emotions at the same time!

I'm not perfect, no one is, and there are days where I don't exercise or eat as well as I could but one thing, I do every single day is that I express my gratitude for this life and for all I have. Life has been tough at times, like it is for everyone, no one is immune from that, but even the things that have broken my heart, losing my parents and our miscarriages, at some level I learnt lessons from all of it. They all taught me the value of gratitude. Life is wonderful but so very fragile and tomorrow is never promised, so all the people in my life whom I love, know how much they mean to me. How do they know this? Because I tell them and more importantly, show them. If we continue to constantly long for or regret what we don't have or have lost then I think we somehow live half a life, instead of appreciating what we have. Expressing gratitude is a way of life and can allow you to view the world through a new lens.

CHAPTER 27

Kindness

Kindness, another core principle of Reiki, is something to share with others while also remembering to be kind to ourselves.

Being kind gives a sense of purpose and creates positive feelings. It connects us with others and it can enhance feelings of self-worth. It's also contagious and I think it's more and more vital in everyday life, especially in these uncertain and unpredictable times. Acts of kindness trigger the release of hormones associated with compassion, the primary one being oxytocin.

Kindness can take many forms, checking up on friends, family members or neighbours to see if they are okay. Complimenting or smiling at someone to brighten their day. Being kind with your words too, you might not always remember exactly what someone has said to you, but you will always remember how those words made you feel.

I believe that the words we say to ourselves though can be the most important and have the most impact. Some of the kindest people I have met seem unable to speak kind words about themselves. Constantly criticising themselves, saying things like *"I am fat"* or *"I am stupid"* or *"I can't do."* Thinking or saying aloud these thoughts can have an extremely negative effect not only on the individual but also on those they live with. The more you keep saying it, the more you give these words power. This then becomes harder to change the mindset and behaviour. It then becomes a habit to criticise yourself. Do you know someone like this or indeed is that someone you? We tend to associate habits as bad, but we can create healthy ones.

I find positive affirmations extremely powerful. I find it useful to say them daily. They don't need to be elaborate, and it may seem strange at first, especially to those who struggle with low self-esteem and self-doubt to verbalise these. Some examples are:

>   *I am loved.*
>   *I am worthy.*
>   *I am enough.*
>   *I am protected.*
>   *I am abundant.*

*

I personally find it best to say these affirmations aloud, the more you practice, the more natural it becomes. The power of it comes in the repetition. The more I said them, the more I started to believe them. Positive affirmations can be a tool to motivate, and they can replace anxious or negative thoughts.

For example, before applying for a new job or going for an interview, instead of saying I won't get this job, or there is no point in going for an interview, its ear marked for someone else. Why not try saying, *"I have all the skills and knowledge required for this role, I am confident in my abilities"* Obviously just saying affirmations on its own won't be enough, there is work required in the completion of the application process and interview preparation if you are shortlisted (and a normal degree of nervousness) but it changes the narrative and is a more positive outlook.

Positive affirmations are not a new concept, some of my favourite songs are affirmations, for example: 'I am what I am', and 'I will survive' by Gloria Gaynor or 'Beautiful' by Christina Aguilera.

So, perhaps if you initially feel too self-conscious in saying positive words aloud, then you can sing them to a feel-good upbeat song.

*

When I made the decision to finally start writing this book, gathering what I had previously written and devoting time to writing regularly, rather than saying *"I am a writer"* I said," *I am a published author", "I have all the words and experiences I need for this book"* It helped in the days where I was stuck, demotivated or when I doubted my abilities. It made me believe that I could do it. Who is going to read this I would often think? I'm not famous nor an expert in anything. I began to think though, of the best-case scenario, that that's perhaps the very reason why people would be drawn to it. I am ordinary, down to earth with a huge desire to help others to help themselves.

Two of my favourite affirmations are, *"I am enough"* and *"I am worthy."* It's something I am passionate about, gently encouraging others to believe that of themselves. For many, it is an extremely difficult concept to realise, perhaps through trauma or being told at some point in their life that they were not good enough. There are so many people who struggle to love themselves never mind letting someone in to love them.

You can even have some affirmations written down in a frame in your room, so you see them when you wake up every day, or on your mirror or perhaps in your hallway, or as your wallpaper on your mobile phone. They can be a visual reminder every day of all that you are and can be. Of course, an individual may need therapy if their self-esteem and mood is so low, but saying these positive words can hopefully help and encourage people to be kinder to themselves. The more you say it, the more you might start believing it.

We have old habits and patterns which we have carried throughout our childhoods and into our adult lives, so it can take time to change your mindset. If you have a goal in mind, something to work towards, an affirmation can strengthen your confidence by reminding you what you can do right now. I struggled at times throughout the years being a stay-at-home mum and then changing career paths and was prone to comparing myself to others. Wondering what people thought, was I able to be anything other than a nurse or a mum? Was I defined by the job I did? Whenever those doubts grew, affirming my worth certainly helped. I am so lucky to have a new purpose after nursing, in helping others heal themselves with Reiki. The question really is, exactly who are we trying to be? We can't compare ourselves to others because there is no one like us in the universe. We are all unique with different skills and talents. We ALL have a purpose and a huge part of feeling content and happy I believe, is finding that purpose and acknowledging our worth.

CHAPTER 28

Reiki

Reiki stimulates the flow of energy and there are many disciplines and cultures which have developed techniques to enhance the flow of energy, including Tai Chi, yoga and acupuncture.

When our energy, (known as Ki or Chi) is low, perhaps due to stress, anxiety, ill health or fatigue, we may feel more negative and find life harder to navigate. Stimulating the flow of energy can bring about subtle or powerful changes resulting in positive alterations in mindset and lifestyle and individuals can feel physically and mentally better after sessions.

Having Reiki 2 was necessary in order for me to become a reiki practitioner and gave me the ability to send distance Reiki. This is a form of energy healing where the energy is sent, transcending time and space, allowing the practitioner/sender to channel Reiki to the recipient regardless of their location. They can experience similar benefits to in person Reiki sessions, such as relaxation, stress reduction and overall well-being.

Five months after completing my Reiki 1, I did Level 2, again with Lorna. Over the course of the next nine months, I offered lots of free sessions for friends, practising on family members and school mums. I started up my own small business from home, Reiki with Catriona Whyte in August 2016, slowly building up a client base.

Reiki practitioners may use a series of hand positions gently on or just above the body and will work intuitively to where they are drawn to. Whilst the reiki will flow to where it is needed regardless of environment, I believe providing a calm space with compassion and empathy are important elements of the practitioner's role as part of the session, and this can impact the client experience enormously. It can be difficult to describe or imagine what a reiki session feels like, so the best way is to experience it for yourself.

There is a growing awareness that Reiki can bring a range of benefits to individuals, some of which include pain relief, reduced levels of stress, improved sleep pattern, a peaceful sense of wellbeing. Some people do not feel much at all whilst others experience heat or cold, tingling or seeing colours. Others may have an emotional release, crying or even laughing. These experiences can be indicators that there is a shift taking place allowing balance and harmony.

There doesn't need to be anything wrong with you, to go for a Reiki session. It can be quite a life changing experience or just an hour of deep relaxation. Some clients do relax, some leave invigorated, focused and others have an emotional release and can feel tired after a session. There are no rights or wrongs, it is your response to the healing that is taking place. No two sessions are ever the same and that is why it can be beneficial to have a few sessions if appropriate, particularly if there is a specific issue, such as anxiety, grief or pain. It should however not be seen as a diagnostic tool and if there are any concerns, then the advice should be for the person to seek medical guidance. During the session the person is fully clothed and generally lying down or seated if preferred.

Some Hospices and cancer wellbeing centres already have Reiki practitioners for their patients, and it is gradually becoming more accepted in hospitals in the the UK, America and Europe. There are scientific studies that have been designed to show its effectiveness. One such study is Connecting Reiki with Medicine, an integrated healthcare project run at St Georges University NHS teaching hospital in London. This is a landmark project hosted by Full Circle Fund Therapies, a complementary therapy charity. It is a three-year trial and the trained Reiki practitioners who are taking part in the study are treating some of the sickest children and adults in areas such as high dependency. Connecting Reiki with Medicine supports research to provide an evidence base for using Reiki in clinical settings. Robust research such as this is integral so that more patients can benefit from it. My hope for the future is one in which Reiki is accessible for all and will be part of a wellbeing service in GP practices, across healthcare and social care settings. Perhaps one day this dream will come true.

I started offering sessions for a local charity called Carers Link in Milngavie in 2018. It is a fantastic organisation which provides information and support to unpaid carers living or caring for someone in East Dunbartonshire. I wanted to do some voluntary Reiki and knowing the benefits of it and having had experience of working with The Prince's Trust in my stroke job, I was drawn to a carer's charity. It wasn't really until I visited patients and their loved ones at home when I was a stroke nurse, that I really appreciated the impact of how being a carer is.

Once or twice a month I would offer Reiki to carers, they were given the opportunity for three sessions. Caring can be extremely demanding physically and mentally. It can be a full-time responsibility, going for a walk, a trip to the shops all must be planned and organised carefully. Carers can be juggling caring for their elderly parents who have a variety of healthcare needs, whilst working and looking after their own family, or they can be parents looking after kids with autism and additional learning needs, or carers looking after spouses or loved ones. The carers who I met this way were so grateful for Reiki, but also just for that time away, an hour where they could relax, have time for self-care. For me, knowing I have held space for them, listening and offering Reiki is a real privilege.

Around the same time, I started to volunteer at my local foodbank once a month. It's a sad indictment of the times that we live in now, that people need the support of these, but they are a lifeline to many. I was involved in making up bags of provisions as an emergency pack for families or individuals for three to four days. There was also a box where people could take things from, which included toilet rolls, sanitary towels, pet food and boxes of biscuits etc.

We live in a world where there is so much food waste and where many must choose between putting food on the table or heating their homes. Where parents may go without, so that their children can eat. When people came to the foodbank, it was important to be welcoming, people can feel a sense of shame at coming there.

There is shame linked with poverty which I find deeply upsetting. In the past, people required foodbanks for a variety of reasons, losing their jobs, addiction issues or relationship breakdowns. Nowadays with the effects of a pandemic and a cost-of-living crisis, they are accessed more and more with families who just can't afford the necessities, many of whom are in full time employment. I stopped volunteering at the foodbank just before the first Covid lockdown, but I can only imagine the need that will have grown since the pandemic.

CHAPTER 29

Believe

I completed my Reiki Master Teacher level in November 2018 with Lorna. I had never really envisaged doing this. I never saw myself as a teacher although there was obviously an element of teaching in nursing with the students in the past. I just knew it was the next step. It really is an honour to pass on the Reiki love and to have my own students who have seen the wonderful benefits it can bring.

I started teaching in 2019 and worried about how it would go; do I know enough? will I be as good as other teachers who have more knowledge and experience than me? But deep down I knew that it's not about that. It's about trusting in myself. It's about being authentic and walking the walk as well as talking the talk.

I am learning all the time, trusting the process and my gut instinct. When I was nursing, I maybe would have struggled to go into detailed explanations of biology and physiology. I never particularly excelled in any passes at school or college or towards the end of my nursing career in gaining a good grade in my university degree, but it never made me any less of a nurse. I never doubted my abilities in what I did, in my competence as a nurse and my ease at caring for others. I knew how to detect signs of changes in a patient's condition and strived to give my patients and their families the highest level of care. That was always good enough for me.

Reiki can be learnt by anyone; it is accessible to all and if you are open to it then the possibilities are endless. Reiki gave me a new vocation and sense of purpose. All those years and experiences of being a nurse were just a chapter of my life. I keep in regular contact with Lorna, my reiki teacher and friend. She is a shining light and guide to many. She is an inspiration to me and to all who meet her. Of course, we are different, but we share many principles and have a deep sense of gratitude for what we do and are humbled by sharing Reiki.

The thing I had missed the most about nursing was the caring for people. I left nursing, but I don't think it ever left me. Now I care in a different way, the principles however, for me, remain the same. Being there for people, the confidentiality aspect and the same sense of privilege in what I do. I realised after undergoing my own journey to a greater self-awareness through counselling, kinesiology and Reiki that the answers are always inside of us. We choose guides and paths sometimes without realising, we make decisions sometimes that we think we regret. I choose now not to do that; the past is exactly that. We make decisions sometimes based on the knowledge we have at that time and the environment, or the age and stage we are at in our lives. In my case I carried a lot of guilt around, at all the things I felt I had done wrong or hadn't done in terms of my mum and dad in their final months. I realise now that everything can be looked at with hindsight and again our perception is exactly that and not always how things really are.

Our experiences are important, our upbringing, our culture, beliefs and they do influence our life but at some stage in our own personal journeys I think it's important to reflect and even challenge these beliefs. Do I really in my heart believe this opinion/ concept to be true or is it someone else's that we have been conditioned to believe? We all have learnt behaviours. Of course, we must teach children, but I think as adult's its healthy to question beliefs and not just blindly accept everything that we are told!

CHAPTER 30

Self-Care

There hasn't just been one thing that helped me and improved my mental health. It's been a variety of things, and each one as important as the next. Self-care and self-development are continuous processes, and I don't believe there are quick fixes. Life will always throw us things that are stressful and challenging, but it is the way in which we learn to cope with them that will guide us through. I don't proclaim this is easy, and I appreciate some people seem to be faced with more adversity than others.

There are many techniques and tools that I have discovered and that I now use on a daily or regular basis. I think it can be overwhelming at times for people to know how to start looking after themselves, and their wellbeing. It's never too early or too late to try and find ways to make our lives happier and calmer. Of course, going to a counsellor or kinesiologist, life coach or complementary therapist costs money but there are also so many ways you can access things for free.

Self- care is not selfish, it is an essential part of looking after our emotional health and wellbeing. Most people now appear to be stressed in some way, constantly busy with juggling work, childcare, looking after elderly parents etc. So many people are tired and feel they need more energy. However, before asking for more energy, you can reflect on who and what you are giving your energy too. Often, energy is thought of something you either lack or never seem to have enough of.

*

Energy:

How you spend your days, the social media you engage with, the programmes you watch and the environments and people you spend time with, all can affect your energy to a significant extent. It is becoming more self-aware and taking positive action to change your small habits that can have the biggest impact. A lot of people, (me included!) claim that they have no time to meditate or be mindful and yet can sit mindlessly scrolling through social media and technology for considerable periods of time. Spending five or ten minutes each day doing a meditation or even making a conscious choice to be more mindful in the everyday tasks that we do, can be so beneficial. Time is our most precious commodity, and we must utilise and embrace it wisely. The human body consists of matter and energy. We are all made up of atoms, molecules, cells and tissues which create our own energy field. When your own connection is healthy, you're more likely to have an abundance of energy. Think of your energy as charging your phone, this gives it a power supply.

Your energy is the same, it needs to be plugged into a source. For me, this source of energy is my own personal daily practice of Reiki on myself. One of the things I began to learn about through Reiki was about our chakras. We have seven main ones, each associated with different organs, emotions and needs. If energy isn't flowing freely then these chakras can become blocked, stagnant energy and illness can then manifest itself. Each chakra has a colour associated with it and corresponds with a layer of the aura. The definition of an aura from the Oxford Dictionary is, the distinctive atmosphere or quality that seems to surround and be generated by a person, thing or place."

The energy that surrounds you can alter your mood, warn you of danger and even provide a gut instinct to leave a room or situation. Everyone can feel auras, for example, walking into a room where the atmosphere is heavy with tension. "You could cut the atmosphere with a knife" is a phrase you often hear. You can feel brighter and happy when in the company of someone who has a warm and welcoming aura, clicking instantly with someone or alternatively, instinctively putting your guard up. Our energetic body picks up any stress or emotions from our environment and our situations and this is reflected in our physical bodies.

There are several techniques you can do to protect your own energy field. You can never really know the people and energies you are going to encounter daily. Cleansing your energy is necessary, just like showering and brushing your teeth. I use a piece of selenite crystal, using sweeping motions from my crown chakra all around and down my body to the floor. I do this in the morning and before going to bed at night. Selenite is known for its purification, cleansing and clearing properties. According to Greek mythology, Selenite was associated with the Goddess of the moon, Selene and that's where the name is derived from.

*

Boundaries:
Does the thought of saying no to people terrify you? Saying no is difficult for many but creating clear personal boundaries is

a form of necessary self-care. Creating effective boundaries, in the context of both your relationships and in your personal and working lives is crucial. They are acceptable behaviours we set for ourselves. Someone with healthy boundaries is able to clearly communicate their wants and needs. It's also though, about accepting other's boundaries and respecting when they say no as well. I had this notion (where it comes from, I'm not entirely clear) of not giving with an expectation to receive. I agree with the principle of this statement, (after all, being kind is about doing something without reward or praise.) However, if we are constantly giving and not receiving, then this can throw us off balance. From personal experience when this happens to me, I then feel taken for granted. Therefore, setting boundaries is so important.

Don't feel guilty about instilling boundaries. Sometimes we need to prioritise ourselves. What do I want, do I really want to spend time with people who are constantly negative or draining? Regardless, of how much someone has annoyed or upset you, it can be therapeutic to look at them or the situation from a place of compassion and love (while keeping the boundary!) Not easy, but a whole lot healthier than being angry or stressed, because you are giving too much of your time and energy to other people, at your own personal expense.

Although I knew what setting personal boundaries meant, putting it into practice was a whole different ball game for me. I struggled at times to disassociate from other people's situations and on reflection I took on a load of other peoples' pain and energy during my nursing career. This was a definite factor in my burnout. I was drained easily by people, situations and environments. It wasn't until Reiki came into my life that I understood this more. I am still empathetic and compassionate. I can put myself in other's shoes, but the difference is I am not walking around wearing them now.

There are many examples I am sure we can all think of where we just felt we couldn't say no to someone. Maybe at times an explanation is required but often, if we are asked to do something we don't want to do, we are allowed to say no without excuses. As someone who can be prone to over-explaining I used to find this difficult. If you are reliable and a people pleaser, then this is a very challenging task. I read only recently, that the word NO is a complete sentence. I have repeated this to many people since who have also found it quite empowering.

CHAPTER 31

Self-Aware

For me, my energy levels started to decrease again in 2021. I lost my get up and go. I couldn't really understand it, I had worked so hard and practiced my self-care but despite this I felt tired and demotivated, even in the spring and summer months. I appreciated we were amid a pandemic, but I know my own body and I just wasn't myself. I started to look at a lot of the symptoms I was experiencing (of which there were many.) Sleepless nights, headaches, tiredness and low mood were only some, but it was the sheer rage I would experience which forced me to address it. The rage would quite literally come from nowhere, usually as a result of Graham or Katie having the audacity to leave something lying around the house or even just express an opinion. I could one minute feel quite serene, floating down from my Reiki zen den upstairs and then literally transform into a wild, unreasonable individual. It was anything but funny and afterwards I would feel ashamed of my over-the-top reactions. I was in fact perimenopausal and looking back on it probably had been for several years.

I began to read books and social media posts from the tireless menopause campaigner, Dr Louise Newson. I researched so many articles and I began using her Balance app to monitor my symptoms. I learnt about how the lack of hormones, oestrogen, progesterone and testosterone can affect so many aspects of the lives of all women. I became empowered by documentaries such as Davina McCall's, and her own personal journey through menopause. All of this gave me the confidence to raise my issues with my GP and make the decision to try Hormone Replacement Therapy (HRT)

My symptoms were by no means as debilitating as I have known others to be, but as I was turning 50 and entering a new chapter in my life, I wanted to be able to to embrace life again. It was becoming a struggle to get out of bed in the morning and I had lost my spark. HRT led to a vast improvement in my sleep pattern and my mood, and our home is, for the most part, back to a calmer place!

Exercising and a healthy diet of course go hand in hand with this. It's been an extremely positive experience so far for me with the HRT, although I know it's not everyone's choice or indeed, many are unable to take it. I am fortunate that I had supportive family and friends who were experiencing similar symptoms that I could talk to. Half of the population will experience menopause and I think it's healthy and fundamental that we continue to discuss and support them through this.

*

Diet and exercise:

Eating healthily is so important. Over the years I've been on a range of diets, they all served a purpose at some stage, kept me focused and helped shed some weight. However, since my mid-forties I decided not to continue. I found them restrictive at times and it was quite disheartening seeing no weight loss or even an increase in my weight, when I had stuck to the advice diligently. Through trial and error, reducing portion control and experimenting with different foods, I feel healthier. My body has changed, I'm not doing a physical job anymore, nor am I running around after a child. I find it harder to lose weight, especially around the mid rift like so many perimenopausal and menopausal woman.

I have also become interested in the correlation between gut health and the mind. There is increasing evidence that a healthy gut equates to a healthy mind. I only recently discovered that seventy per cent of our immunity is in our gut. When I was nursing, doing shift work and not eating in a particularly healthy way, with all the highly processed foods, chippies and alcohol, I suffered from irritable bowel symptoms. I would have crippling stomach cramps and diarrhoea often. I love food though and that's not changed. However, I feel I have a healthier relationship with it now. I don't emotionally eat the same way that I used to, and I am much more aware of portion control and understanding that my body and mind can feel more sluggish because of overindulgence or not eating healthily. I finally came to to the conclusion in my forties that I had indeed got my numbers round the wrong way. The 80/20 rule did not mean 80 per cent eating and drinking whatever I liked and the other 20 per cent eating healthily!

Exercise is also so important for our overall health and wellbeing. Exercising in a gym environment isn't for everyone and it doesn't need to be. There are many exercise classes in church halls or out in nature. For me, a daily walk outside provides not only the physical benefits in moving my body but also mentally and emotionally to the connection with nature.

Being outdoors, in amongst the trees, immersing yourself in the forest atmosphere, using all five senses, is extremely therapeutic.

Shinrin-yoko or forest bathing is a Japanese term and was first developed in the 1980s following scientific studies conducted by their government. Studies showed that mindful exploration in a forest could reduce blood pressure, lower cortisol and improve concentration and memory. The study also found that trees release chemicals which boost the immune system. So, there is actual scientific evidence that hugging trees is good for you- don't knock it until you have tried it!

I am extremely fortunate to have easy access to green spaces where I live. I think everyone gained a deeper appreciation for nature over these past challenging years. The physical and mental health benefits of mindful walking and being in nature are enormous and well documented. It is important to stay active and not be too sedentary which of course can be difficult due to the increase of people now working from home and other lifestyle and health factors. There is increasing evidence of health problems associated with sitting for long periods. It is thought that it slows down the body's metabolism, which in turn affects its ability to regulate blood sugar, blood pressure and break down body fat.

*

Meditation and the breath:

Meditation is another tool and part of a way of life for many people. Gelong Tubten is a Buddhist monk and a pioneer in mindfulness meditation teaching. His journey and his experience are fascinating and inspiring. I had the pleasure of hearing him speak at a wellbeing event in Edinburgh in early 2020 and I found him so charismatic, genuine and wise. I drew inspiration from his book "The Monks Guide to Happiness" as it gives guidance, exercises and techniques we can use for meditation/ mindfulness, getting started and realistic ways to build it into a regular practice.

Breathing is fundamental, not just in meditation or in relaxation but in daily living. It is something we do naturally, probably without much thought, but the breath is so important. I only became aware of this when I suffered from anxiety. In the past, when I was anxious, especially when driving in an unfamiliar area I would hold my breath and tense my whole body. Home visits as a stroke nurse were a nightmare, sweaty palms gripped onto the steering wheel for dear life.

I occasionally do the breath holding now when driving, and I try my best to avoid motorways, but the difference is that I am aware of it immediately. I began to practice breathing when I was calm, I did this regularly. Then, when I was exposed to a stressful situation or became anxious, I could automatically slow things down and I relaxed. I know that if I am stressed, my thoughts can run away with me and so can my speech. So just taking that minute to be aware, slowing down and concentrating on the breath can be transformative. I am now mindful every day of my breath. There are so many health benefits and a growing awareness that deep breathing can be an effective intervention to help improve stress and chronic health conditions. Breathing in through the nose and out through the mouth. There are many techniques which can be adopted and plenty of information and tips on a variety of social platforms. In recent years I have also seen an increase in breathwork training and workshops which can be transformative for people.

*

Over the years, reading positive and spiritual books, using affirmations and expressing gratitude are things that helped me heal and become more self-aware. Realising that all the things the experts advise on, like being in nature, eating healthily, exercising and being mindful do have positive effects. They are so important for our mental and physical wellbeing. I have gained insights and wisdom from books, people and teachers. It is also important to recognise that self-care and healing is an ongoing process.

CHAPTER 32

Forgiveness

One of the chapters in Gelong Tubtens book was on forgiveness. Much is said and written about the need and power of forgiveness. I tended to associate that with forgiving other people but what I learnt after reading this, was the importance of forgiving myself. For such a long period, probably for twenty-five years or so, I had carried a lot of guilt about my mum dying and not looking after her at home or spending quality time with her during her final weeks and months. These feelings of guilt would crop up every now and again. It didn't consume me but nonetheless it was there. I did discuss this at counselling with Jan and I tried to understand it but still the guilt clung to me. Not being physically present in my mum's final moments weighed heavily on me. However, around the same time as reading about forgiveness, both for myself and others, I had conversations with my Kinesiologist and a friend that completely changed my perspective.

All during my nursing career when looking after patients who were dying, the most worrying thing for their loved ones was the fear of them being alone at the very end of their life. I wasn't present for either of my parents when they took their last breaths, physically holding their hands, so I understood those concerns. When someone we love is dying it's only natural to want to be with them and if we are not, it can leave those left behind with a tremendous sense of guilt. We tend to focus on the last hours and moments of life but what about the months and years of life we shared with these people we love? Claire, at one of my sessions suggested that I had been looking at the situation purely from my own perspective, that of an eighteen-year-old. Also, I was neglecting the fact that I didn't have time to process the grief from losing my dad before being propelled into more grief with my mum. She put across another viewpoint to me, that of my mum's. She suggested that perhaps my mum understood the normal need for freedom and enjoying myself as a teenager, maybe she wanted me to go out, to live my teenage life. Maybe she did not want me to be her carer, that was a bit of a lightbulb moment for me!

Shortly after this appointment with Claire, I had a conversation with a dear friend called June who was dying. We always met up with other friends but this one and only time it was just me and her. We chatted and reminisced as we always did about our Ward 17 days, and she spoke about her teenage son whom she would be leaving behind. She didn't want him to see her in pain and she wanted him to know she would always be there looking down on him. She wanted him to go on and enjoy his life and be happy. That afternoon will stay with me forever, not just because I was humbled that she shared this with me but because it allowed me to finally forgive myself. Now, when a lot of my friend's kids turn eighteen, I think "Catriona, you did so well to cope with all of this at such a young age."

June was part of a trio, the three amigos, Norma, June and Joan, and I was fortunate to be a part of their friendship on many occasions in the last year or so of June's life. I will never forget one Friday afternoon, meeting up with them at the Beatson Oncology Centre in Glasgow, where June was an inpatient. We sat in her room and chatted and laughed, but it was not just a sharing of coffee and cakes but of love, friendship and compassion. That feeling of love and kindness in the room was palpable and I will cherish it forever. There were a few similarities with June and my mum, they were the same age, both dying from cancer and both spending their last days/week of life in a hospice. Both grateful for the life they had been given and for the care they had received. June spent her last few days in a hospice with a view of the Campsie Hills which she was so grateful for. It reminded her of her childhood with her grandparents and at some level offered her a sense of peace by the view of nature she had. I miss June's friendship, sense of humour and kindness.

CHAPTER 33

Joy

I believe as important as being mindful, exercising and being in nature are, there is also a need to spark joy into everyday life. Joy to me is like a euphoric happiness. There have been many momentous occasions where I have experienced it: my wedding day, the day Katie was born, moving back to Scotland to name a few. There are so many more moments though in the everyday. Playing with my dog Max, sledging with Katie, dancing and singing, the sun shining and the magical feeling when I am teaching Reiki. What joyous occasions can you recall in the big and small moments?

Fun and laughter should never be underestimated and sparking joy I believe; is an important feeling we should factor into our lives more often. Why do we think when we grow up and become responsible (or not) that we have to stop having fun? There are so many ways to spark joy, but I am sure most people would agree that laughter can sometimes be the best medicine. How do you feel after a right good belly laugh? What or who makes you laugh out loud? Nowadays with stress seeming such a normal part of everyday life and the constant stream of tragic and sad news we have been bombarded with, the pandemic, war, poverty and the cost-of-living crisis, it is more important now than ever to try and find joy in something.

You often hear of the importance of bringing out your inner child. What did you enjoy doing as a child before the stresses and worries of adulthood began? There is so much joy in kids, being in their company. We all love the sound of a baby or young child laugh, we encourage it, it's infectious.

Speaking to grandparents, in general there is an appreciation of having more time, of being in the moment with them and of course for most, the ability to hand the children back to their parents. Katie has a lovely relationship with Grahams parents, and they are always so interested in what's going on in Katie's life as well as in all their other grandchildren lives too. Graham's Auntie Sheila described what being a grandparent is like:

> *"Being a mum presents many challenges, most of which involve juggling your time and learning how to cope with parenting situations as they arise, very often for the first time and not always sure you're getting it right. Living life in the fast lane with not enough hours in the day to allow you to stop, breathe and enjoy the moment. Before you know it, if you are lucky enough, you become a granny and life takes on a whole new meaning. You can stay in the park that extra 10 minutes, bedtime can happily be extended so they can ask you again and again to finish reading stories or recounting yours from the seemingly old days."*

CHAPTER 34

The Sound of Music

Dancing and singing evokes a lot of joy for me. I still love music of all genres, especially rock, country and popular music. There are so many benefits of music, everything has a vibration, some notes will deeply resonate and are pleasant, while others can agitate or just not feel good. Musical preference is a personal choice and where would we be without it? Music can instantly transport us back to happy or sad times in our lives. We can relive those memories when songs that are meaningful to us are played. What's your go to song that makes you feel good, that ignites your passion or just makes you smile? Why not get the music on and as we say in Glasgow, *"Gie it Laldy!"*

I have my go to playlist for motivation and inspiration and when I want a wee push then I turn to one of my favourites, St Elmo's Fire. Even though I've only watched the movie once, for some reason, the song just resonates, I feel unstoppable and empowered after I listen to it.

*

Sound is healing and the more formal practice of sound healing is something that allows you to enter a deep state of relaxation using therapeutic instruments. There are many variations, one to one or group sessions, both enabling you to bathe in the vibrations, guiding your body into a state of balance. We will all have benefitted from sound healing on a regular basis in our daily lives. Perhaps playing a soothing playlist or podcast or listening to the beating drum of the rainfall.

It was only recently I that I had my first experience of a sound bath. I was transported deep into the jungle, with the sounds of the river Amazon, weaving my way through the seasons and vibrations beating loudly in my heart as well as my mind. It was an incredible experience of sounds like a finely tuned orchestra and beautifully directed by the conductor Tommy from the Sonic Den in Glasgow.

I sang in a church choir for years when I was at secondary school and really loved it. I was a soloist and wouldn't think much of singing in front of hundreds of people. It helped my confidence and I have fond memories of being part of it, especially at Midnight Mass on Christmas Eve. I realised several years ago that I really missed singing and decided to join a rock choir. I did enjoy elements of it but felt it wasn't particularly for me. So, for just now I am back to belting out some tunes and dancing at my solo kitchen discos.

CHAPTER 35

Finding Meaning Through the Chaos

The year 2020 brought a challenge to everyone across the globe with the Covid-19 pandemic, none more so than the NHS. I can't begin to contemplate what it must have felt like for the staff who worked in all health and social care settings, and I empathised hugely with nursing home staff who had many of their residents die, sometimes having journalists camped out outside.

Although Nursing has changed dramatically over the years since I qualified in 1993, I hope the essence remains the same, that of caring. I am aware that there is immense pressure on health and social care staff, now more than ever, with financial constraints, staffing and resource pressures. What hasn't changed is that in some care environments, professionals are dealing daily with traumatic and stressful situations. To be on the front line and witness multiple deaths must have a cumulative effect. There is a societal assumption that there is an inbuilt resilience, and that it's part of the job, but we must look for ways to care for the ones who care for others. Most nurses now work 12-hour shifts, certainly in the hospital setting, some depleted and compassion fatigued, breaktimes a luxury when in fact they should be a necessity. I would never put anyone off applying for nursing as I loved the years that I spent there but it is a changed profession. We also need to change the narrative of how we regard older people in society. There is a tendency for them to be regarded as a burden and a drain on our services. They can be labelled as bed blockers in hospitals, none of which is their fault, but a resource issue at social care level. This is by no means a new concept but undoubtedly a worrying crisis. Care workers need to feel valued, financially as well as personally for the work that they do. During the Covid-19 pandemic the staff in hospitals and community settings were faced daily with I'm sure, their own fear and that of the patients or clients they cared for. I had several friends desperate to see their dying loved ones, knowing that they would only live for a short time. The unimaginable pain of not being able to touch and hold their family members close.

I regard myself as one of the lucky ones, my family and close friends all remained in good health. I certainly value my health even more deeply now and I don't take it for granted. During the pandemic I found myself thinking about my dad more and more and how life must have been for him, as a relatively young man, in his final years of illness. It made me think of how long it had been since I had seen or held my parents, for so many people they would get that opportunity eventually, but I wouldn't, and it just magnified the grief and years that have passed. I was initially frustrated at not being able to do anything to help others but yet somewhat relieved I didn't have to put myself or my family at risk by nursing. I did, however, help in my own way with offering distance Reiki.

I had a deep sense of honour in relation to those friends, family members and clients who trusted me with their fears, traumas and challenges during these difficult times. I knew some friends and family members who had been been ill and experiencing emotional distress. I am glad they felt the benefit and the power of Reiki. So many people I have seen online or in person look physically better after Reiki, like a weight has been lifted from their shoulders and minds. As it is a natural healing energy, it can be used alongside medical treatments.

If you decide to learn how to practice Reiki, it's so important to do it regularly on yourself. I became more even more aware of this during the past few years. I was giving a lot to others but not enough to myself. I now regularly do a distance Reiki exchange with my friend Maureen as well as hosting and attending Reiki shares. The shares are invaluable and are a meeting of likeminded folk who come together to give and receive this wonderful healing energy.

Lockdown also led me to learning about crystals. I had always admired them, their colours and shapes but never really understood their healing powers. I did several online crystal workshops and began my Crystal Level 1 and 2 training, enabling me to be becoming a crystal practitioner. I was taught by the wonderful Caroline Swinburne.

The concept of crystal healing has been around for centuries, but it has come to the forefront more in recent years with the easier accessibility to them and the trends in social media which have propelled them into becoming more mainstream. Crystal healing involves using gemstones to bring balance to a person's body and mind. Individual crystals are known for their own special energies that can help in all different areas of someone's life. Crystals themselves don't need to only be used in a crystal healing session with a practitioner. They can also be worn as jewellery or used in areas of your home or workspace.

*

Although I gained these wonderful new skills during the pandemic, the most important thing to me was the precious time I got to spend with Katie. Graham and I have taught her that you can experience many different emotions at the same time. Being strong is not about putting on a brave face, a stiff upper lip. It is about understanding we are all human and we all have times in our lives where it feels like it's too much. I am grateful that she is open and honest about her feelings. I hope this continues through the teenage years and beyond. It has been such a different story for so many adolescents. I felt for young people during this time, not being amongst their peers, many with stressful and perhaps volatile home lives. I believe it is fundamental to start early with children on strategies and tools to help them with their well-being, introducing mindfulness, breathwork, expressing gratitude etc. So many people I have known have had children, mainly teenagers who have struggled with their mental health and particularly anxiety. Social media has created a desire for instant gratification, there seems to be an impatience (not necessarily confined to teenagers and young adults) of wanting things now and not being able to wait. There is no doubt that children nowadays are under more pressure than before, and yet they are a generation that is awakening to the realities of global warming and other key environmental issues. My own daughter is educating me on these crucial topics.

Although times have changed and not always for the better, I am hopeful that we are becoming a society in which your sexuality, heritage and gender doesn't matter. I don't know all the answers but what I feel strongly, is the need for us not to wait until there is an issue with children but give them the necessary tools from a young age that may help them navigate their way through their life. It is vital to teach them the value of kindness and gratitude, of being mindful. A calm mind is as important as one with a lot of knowledge.

I also think we should never underestimate how children feel. We need to let them grow and build resilience, making mistakes along the way. It's so important to listen. It always angered me when I was a teenager or going into my twenties when people criticised or made assumptions that I was only a wee lassie. I found it extremely condescending, and I remember a conversation I had with a friend's mum who laughed at me when I said that I had been feeling stressed, I was around twenty-two at the time. It always stuck with me, and I would never assume anyone's life is stress or worry free. Just because you're young doesn't mean you don't have stresses in life. You might not have the wisdom that perhaps comes with getting older, but you can have many experiences in life like I did, that you didn't want or choose, but make you grow up quickly.

CHAPTER 36
Embracing Life's Seasons

Until the winter of 2020 I realised that I had approached every autumn and winter with a sense of dread, especially since my breakthrough. During lockdown though something shifted, I completed a seasonal writing course during the pandemic which included lots of information about Traditional Chinese and Western medicine. I learnt so much about nature, seasonal foods and that there are certain emotions attached to each season. Apparently in Autumn the emotion associated with that season is grief. That was another lightbulb moment for me, thirty years down the line. It made sense, all those years of feeling intense unresolved grief during the autumn months. At this point, I realised that in actual fact the winter months were not as challenging as the autumn ones for me, which changed my mindset.

I became aware of how I am more in sync with the seasons, and I developed a greater understanding and appreciation of nature and animals. Many plants and animals hibernate in winter and although things may look empty or even bleak in the gardens and parks, underneath the surface, the plants and animals are being nurtured, resting and preparing to re-emerge in spring. I realised that my body and mind is working in tandem with the seasons. Keeping warm, conserving vital energy, and allowing myself to go deep within. It has always been in the winter months that I sowed the seeds for growth, physically, emotionally and spiritually. I began to appreciate that it is ok and indeed natural to be more contemplative in winter and necessary to prepare for the months ahead. This was a powerful realisation for me.

There are also so many things I realised that I really love in the winter, the cold, crisp and foggy mornings, watching the flurries of snowflakes and having fun in snowball fights and sledging with my daughter. There is a joy in letting go, being childlike again and I love hearing the shrieks of laughter cascading down the hills from families all around. Not even a global pandemic stopped that fun. I love log fires, watching the flames dance and the crackling sounds which seems to ignite a flame within me, yet a stillness too. I love the feeling of cosiness at home, a place where I am safe and loved. Coorie is a Scottish word traditionally meaning to snuggle or cuddle but to me it means not just appreciating the warmth from the fire but from the love that surrounds me from my family.

I looked at the world around me differently, changing my former bleak mindset to saying that winter has become my in-between season. Instead of focusing on the things I didn't like, I embraced the ones I did. At last, I have acknowledged and accepted my low mood and decreased motivation during the autumn months after decades of not understanding it or fighting against it. I have now decided to practice the pause through the winter months. Life of course goes on for people, work, looking after homes and families but learning more about the four seasons has helped me understand myself more and also the world around me.

I see the winter season with fresh eyes now, I plant the seeds, rest when I can, restore and patiently wait for my favourite season to come, spring. I am now always thankful for the gifts that winter can bring. Rather than a sense of foreboding I can now look forward to future winters with a greater understanding and perspective.

Even the word spring excites me. It gives me a feeling of hope and an eager anticipation of what may be, it energises and inspires me, I feel the fog starting to lift. Spring is the season I love the most. The month of March heralds the ending of my hibernation and the promise of fresh beginnings. Cherry blossoms are a springtime spectacle that symbolises a time of renewal. Just round the corner from me, a street is lined with them and when the gentle winds blow these beautiful flowers fall like confetti. This season brings energy to my body and mind, and I have a deep sense of gratitude for that. I am grateful to feel that euphoria again. I look at things with fresh eyes, the daffodils, the tulips, they are all signs of rebirth and hope. They come every year and yet the joy I find in those sunny mornings, the eager anticipation and the belief that something wonderful is about to happen, as if I am seeing things for the first time. I am grateful for the increase in energy and motivation, and I am now aware and grateful for the sense of hibernation throughout the winter months. Fresh ideas come and I look forward to making plans.

*

My SAD symptoms are not as prevalent now, and although my mood dips, it's not the same as the overwhelming sadness and sometimes despair that I used to experience. I now generally just feel quite demotivated and have a lack of oomph. Lockdown allowed us all to appreciate the seasons in general, as we paid more attention to them than ever before. I witnessed nature in all its wonder, day by day, month by month, season by season. Although I don't like the way that Autumn makes me feel, I now see the beauty in it and know it's like everything, it's temporary. It is a stunning season in terms of all the autumnal colours. One of my favourite memories as a child is crunching through the dazzling red, amber and yellow leaves in the Queens Park with my mum. I loved doing this with Katie when she was young too. I love summer also, although I can often be heard complaining of being too hot. I love the longer hours of daylight and even when my hours of sleep may be less due to the heat overnight, I am able to cope, and I don't have the same lack of energy that comes with the autumn and winter months.

*

Many people live with SAD to varying degrees and I would encourage them to invest in a lightbox and be outdoors as much as possible in natural sunlight and exercise regularly. My symptoms are much improved with the tools I now have. These feelings and the sluggishness last until near Christmas and then I seem to get a push to get organised and ready for the festive period. This has always been the same for my whole adult life but the difference now, is that I don't say I suffer from SAD but that I live with it. I use my lightbox daily and try not to eat too many carbohydrates as that enhances my already sluggish feeling and brain fog and is something that people with SAD can crave.

I understand the need to be outdoors and in natural sunlight as much as possible. I take Vitamin D over the autumn and winter months and increase certain foods such as oily fish and eggs which provide Vitamin D as we don't make enough Vitamin D from sunlight during the autumn and winter months. I start using my lightbox early September time, give myself regular Reiki and have early nights and get daily exercise. These tools are non-negotiable for me. It helps, they work, and my mental health needs them. I still feel depleted easily, but I can usually get myself together for Christmas. Then I look forward to January. Despite it being a long month, generally cold and wet, I feel it's a new year and a new start and that I have gotten through the autumn season.

I struggled sometimes with motivation in lockdown towards exercise. In the beginning, it was different, the sun shone most days, and as we were only allowed to go out for a walk once a day, we seemed to embrace this golden hour. It became an opportunity and a pleasure to discover new woodland walks. By the end of the year 2020 and the beginning of 2021 though as the weather grew colder and the grey skies descended, I became like many, covid weary and lost the daily momentum somewhat, also the perimenopause didn't help. However, this time I didn't berate myself, I just acknowledged how I felt and knew I would emerge again with the promise of spring.

CHAPTER 37

Max

The summer of 2021 was life changing for me and our family when we became dog owners to our boy Max, a handsome, black Labrador. The early morning daily walks in the natural sunlight improved my mental health considerably during the autumn and winter months and without doubt has been a game changer for me. Like many people during the pandemic, we began to toy with the idea of getting a dog. It wasn't something I had ever really considered. I hadn't grown up with animals and we only ever had had goldfish that we had won at fairs. Graham and Katie were extremely keen, and I was reluctant. I knew it would be me that would be doing most of the walking and looking after any pet might be restrictive. They began to talk about it all the time though, especially on our walks together and even started to name this dog we hadn't got yet and practice how they would speak to it. I eventually caved in and suggested a family meeting to discuss tactics, breeds etc. Graham listened to Katie and I and then said he would only really consider a Labrador. Case closed!

A family friend Janette bred labradors so we knew it would be coming from good stock. Lots of phone calls were made to Graham's dad Iain (who was a vet) and research ensued. Graham had grown up with two labs, Susy and Shona, so this was the reason why he was so keen on getting a labrador. Max's mum had four puppies on the 31st of May 2021. It was an exciting time, going to Aberdeenshire to meet them. It was so hard choosing one as they were all adorable. We chose the one that seemed to be the shyest. First impressions most definitely aren't quite what they seem! The anticipation of him coming was something to look forward to in a time where there wasn't much else to be excited about. We met Max when he was a few weeks old, and we returned to take him home mid-August when he was around ten weeks.

It was a beautiful sunny day and a stressful three-hour journey back to Glasgow ensued. Max was panting and hot and I was terrified. We got him home and it reminded me of all those years ago when we placed Katie in the living room, thinking what on earth do we do now? Graham had the weekend off and Katie was off for a few days before starting secondary school. I think it was perfect timing as it took her mind off the transition from primary to secondary school. She had never even been in the actual school yet due to restrictions and had missed out on the induction days like so many others.

In the early weeks and months of looking after Max, I found it quite stressful, all new and honestly overwhelming. As we got him when restrictions had eased, and had only recently started to see people again, I found the staying in before he got his twelve-week vaccinations quite challenging. Knowing it was only for a short period helped. Right from the start, Max was jumpy, bitey and gorgeous. After the chewing of the furniture and carpets stopped, I started to enjoy him more.

*

Graham had found it difficult writing Christmas cards after our miscarriages, as two of our babies were due in early December. He found himself wanting to write a fourth name, I remembered this when I wrote Christmas cards in 2022. Max is now that fourth member and he has completed our family. He was the missing piece in the jigsaw, and I feel his coming into our lives finally gave me acceptance of Katie being an only child and all our losses. He has been therapy for me which I didn't even know I needed. Like everything else in life, you learn to adapt and the joy he has brought individually and collectively to our family is simply beyond measure. I am besotted and in love with my fur baby. Yes, I know he is a dog and not a child, but he is my boy. He is my companion, and I know we will look after each other in the years and adventures to come. There is something in the way he looks at me, it touches my soul. It was the best thing we did even though I was so reluctant to begin with. It has also been a godsend for getting me out for walks every day, hail, rain or shine, something living in Scotland we are well used too!

The welcome I receive every time I walk in the room is beyond compare. Even if me and Max have a falling out, it doesn't last long, it's forgotten about, and we move on. With the puppy dog eyes you can't stay mad at him for long. He, of course does rule the roost and although some initial ground rules we have managed to maintain, like not being allowed upstairs, the not being allowed on the couch rule was broken after six months. I vowed it would never happen, but life is too short, and we all love cuddling into him. I never fully understood the whole pets being part of the family idea, but it didn't take too long for me to love this beautiful and loyal dog. He has been medicine for the soul for us all.

CHAPTER 38

This is me

My depression and anxiety were around grief and loss, and it took me a long time to understand that coming to terms with these things is a long process. You don't ever get over grief but learn to live with it. It's not a straight road and you can't take short cuts. You can drive along at a steady pace sometimes, within the speed limit and then, suddenly and unexpectedly, something will cause you to stop abruptly, like a speed bump and it hits you with a force that is indescribable.

Just as I hadn't processed my parents' loss, I don't think I really acknowledged my grief over our miscarriages. At some level I became guilty again as I felt that I already had so much. Living this Reiki life and with practising gratitude being at the forefront of my daily practice, I buried the grief. At some point though, you must stop and validate how you feel. You are allowed to cry, be angry and ask questions. I would say this to many and yet struggled to do this myself.

Lorna, my Reiki Master and teacher made me realise this after a session with her.

"I notice you always say I think, rather than I feel." So, I began to allow myself to feel, to cry, to grieve, to feel cheated and sad for the babies I never had, to feel envious of others. This for me was yet another reminder, that we can feel seemingly opposite things at the same time. I felt sad and grateful, and it helped me to move forwards and accept the things that had happened to me in my life.

I was told regularly that I was so strong, resilient and a good role model and leader. Although this was said with the best of intentions it probably encouraged me to put more pressure on myself to be brave and strong and positive all the time, but that isn't possible. I realise now that its ok not to be ok and I am conscious now when I say these positive and powerful adjectives to describe someone who is living through grief or distress, that I follow it up with, its ok and indeed necessary to feel how you feel.

I think about death often, because I understand the fragility of life after losing my parents so young, the experiences in my nursing career and of course as I am now in my sixth decade. Getting older (and the gratitude for that in itself) and being married to a palliative medicine consultant who works in a hospice, also puts things in perspective.

I often think we cannot quite believe how others cope with traumatic life changing events and yet we get through them ourselves and we somehow find the strength from somewhere. I have known friends and family who have been through so much trauma with their children from mental illness and life-threatening conditions and the unimaginable pain of grief in losing a child. It is so true that people may be living and facing battles that we know nothing about, so it's important to be mindful of that and to be kind always.

*

I accept now, that for whatever reason another child was not meant to be for us. The hope is no longer there due to my age, and I couldn't imagine having a toddler to run around with, having a puppy has been exhausting enough. However, I know that it was hope that kept me going for all those years. Of course, I have a sadness, that will never leave me, it is a part of me just like the loss of my mum and dad, except I could speak about them freely. Miscarriage is a grief of a different kind. You have never met this baby, held it or watched it grow but in that short period of time there can be so many dreams and plans. We had so much love in our hearts to offer. It was not just a deep desire to have another child, but it was also for Katie to have a sibling. It was only recently during the pandemic that we told Katie about the miscarriages. I just couldn't have had that conversation before. It was the right time. It's not that it was a big secret, she was so young when it all happened, but at some level I wanted her to know that we tried so hard for her to be a big sister. She has given us so much love and joy and we are grateful for her and the gift of parenthood every day, a privilege which is denied to many.

Another part of my acceptance was acknowledging all the things that I had achieved since my miscarriages. There were things I may not have done if I had had another child. Becoming a Reiki practitioner and teacher, the time I invested in myself for self-care, setting up my business and writing this book. Acceptance allows me to move forward, remembering the children I never got to hold but thankful I was given the opportunity to be a mum. I was fortunate enough to be a stay-at-home mum and I have appreciated that more and more as the years have gone by. I never wished Katie's life away. It was really becoming a mum that let me live in the moment, to be present and to enjoy each milestone she reached. Perhaps at some level I knew as the years went by that Katie would be an only child and so every school show, every Christmas, every birthday and special occasion I relished every moment.

Being vulnerable and honest is brave and I have wanted to be authentic whilst respecting other people. This process has been cathartic, I have cried, laughed and reflected so much. There is courage in vulnerability, and I believe I have faced many things with courage.

*

The answers are always inside of us, if we can find ways to listen to our bodies and minds. To trust ourselves and respond. I always wanted to make a difference, I have helped people in my role as a nurse, in my voluntary roles, as a Reiki Practitioner and now I hope in my role as a writer. Reaching out to others, encouraging them to believe in themselves and their worth and to have gratitude for the gifts in this life is part of my life's purpose.

Even when challenged and faced with adversity we can all find glimmers of light, of joy, of hope and even fun. Life is for living and how we manage to deal with all its challenges, can determine how happy our lives are. There is always hope and always something to be grateful for.

Acknowledgements

My Family

With love and gratitude to my mum and dad for the happy and loving childhood they gave me. I hope I've made you proud. To my sisters Christine and Yvonne for the memories we have shared together throughout our lives. Christine, as the eldest, stepped into the role of our parents and did so much for us all. Yvonne provided tremendous assistance while I wrote my memoir, with her incredible memory for dates, and we enjoyed reminiscing about the past. To my amazing nieces Laura and Rachel, I'm proud of you both for all you have achieved so far.

To Graham for loving and supporting me all through the years, you are my rock. To Katie, you are a source of pure love and happiness in our life. I love you and your dad to the moon and back.

With love and gratitude to Graham's parents, Anne and Iain, for being the best in laws and to all his extended family, in particular Sheila George for her proofreading and loving feedback.

*

Friends

Friendships have played a crucial role in my life as is evident from my story.

A special thanks to my nursing friends from the class of August 1990: Lindsay, Sheila, Michelle, Mags, Brenda, Wilma, Elaine, Carol Anne, Cheryl, Fiona and Susan. So many happy memories with you all.

*

Heartfelt thanks to Lindsay who sat next to me, all those years ago, on our first day of college. We became instant best buddies and we have always supported each other. During the early stages of my grief and depression, you had a sense of knowing when to encourage me to face the world and when to respect my need for solitude. You still do. It's a joy now to see Katies friendship with your beautiful daughter Elizabeth and son Finlay.

*

To Mags McCall for your kindness and compassion throughout my stay in Wirral and throughout my fertility and miscarriage journey. For your belief and enthusiasm in writing my memoir and being the first person, I shared it with.

*

To Elaine Close, who now lives in Australia, I miss your chat and sense of fun. Your support, especially during my anxiety was filled with love and kindness.

*

To Brenda Bryceland for the meaningful moments, we've shared, and in particular during our time in Ward 17. Your support during Christine's illness and treatment and through the years has meant a great deal to me.

*

To Wilma Conning, for your deep understanding of my homesickness during my time in Wirral and your continued love and friendship. Thankfully we now live in much closer proximity to each other.

*

To Carol Anne Barbour, our bond was forged as student nurses on placement all those years ago and we have remained close friends ever since. We have supported each other in our grief but also in our happy times.

*

To Colette Farrington, Susan Crumlish and Tracy Docherty, heartfelt thanks for the fun times we have shared since we were at school. Long may they continue.

*

Thank you to all the mums I met and the friends they became during my time in Wirral and on our return to Scotland, especially to Siobhan McManus. Fridays certainly became more feel good with you and your daughter Emma.

*

To Maureen Annan, thank you for the time and detailed attention you dedicated to proofreading and editing my book, and for your friendship and Reiki exchanges.

*

To Gill McKay for your guidance and wisdom, a fellow self-published author who is also passionate about inspiring and encouraging others.

*

To the patients and their families whom I cared for throughout my nursing career. I cherish all the experiences whether positive or otherwise. I am still humbled by the stories you shared.

To all the staff I worked with, many of whom became great friends. We worked many crazy and stressful shifts, but that sense of camaraderie and loyalty is undoubtedly what kept me so enthusiastic and passionate about my job. I am forever grateful for the many close friendships and love they brought into my life.

*

To the clients and friends with whom I share the gift of Reiki. Thank you for your trust.

*

To Kim and Sinclair Macleod from Indie Authors World for your support and guidance through the process of publishing my memoir.

About the Author

Catriona Whyte is a Reiki Master Teacher and Practitioner, who lives in the outskirts of Glasgow with her husband, daughter and dog Max.

She was a nurse in the NHS for eighteen years, a profession she found equally rewarding and challenging. The discovery of Reiki at a Holistic event in 2007, propelled her into a journey of self-awareness on a deeply personal and spiritual level.

Her passion is sharing this healing modality with empathy and kindness, fostering a community where people can heal and evolve within a safe, supportive and nurturing environment.

Printed in Great Britain
by Amazon